LOGIC
BASIS C

Oxford University Press, Ely House, London W. 1

GLASGOW   NEW YORK   TORONTO   MELBOURNE   WELLINGTON
CAPE TOWN   IBADAN   NAIROBI   DAR ES SALAAM   LUSAKA   ADDIS ABABA
DELHI   BOMBAY   CALCUTTA   MADRAS   KARACHI   LAHORE   DACCA
KUALA LUMPUR   SINGAPORE   HONG KONG   TOKYO

ISBN 0 19 824157 7

LOGIC AND THE
BASIS OF ETHICS

BY

ARTHUR N. PRIOR

Lecturer in Philosophy
Canterbury University College, New Zealand

OXFORD
AT THE CLARENDON PRESS

*For which of you, intending to build
a tower, sitteth not down first, and
counteth the cost, whether he have
sufficient to finish it?*

LUKE 14: 28

First published 1949
Reprinted 1956, 1961, 1965, 1968, and 1975

*Printed in Great Britain
at the University Press, Oxford
by Vivian Ridler
Printer to the University*

CONTENTS

INTRODUCTION

THE aim of the present series of studies is to clarify a certain issue in moral philosophy. The issue is, roughly, this: We all sometimes describe conduct and character (and perhaps other things; but we shall not here be concerned with other things) as 'good' or 'bad', or as 'right' or 'wrong'. Some hold that there is nothing out of the ordinary about what these words refer to—that they either merely express the feelings of the person using them, or refer to some 'natural' characteristic of the objects to which they are applied, such as their conduciveness or otherwise to biological survival. Those who take such a view are generally called 'naturalists'. Others hold that ethical predicates—words like 'good' and 'evil', 'right' and 'wrong'—represent qualities which are *sui generis*, in a category on their own, different from all 'natural' qualities. These others we may call, in the meantime, anti-naturalists.

I aim to clarify this issue, not to settle it; and in my view one of the main factors which have made the issue obscure is the illusion of some anti-naturalists that purely logical considerations can settle it. These writers have claimed, in other words, that the anti-naturalist position is capable of proof; a claim which I think it is quite impossible to make good, and which has only served to make it more difficult to understand what the anti-naturalist position is. Being an anti-naturalist myself, I regard this as unfortunate. Naturalists, at the same time, have contributed their share to the confusion by plain inconsistency, usually by trying to combine their naturalism with uses of moral terms which only the opposite position could justify. But while the present work is directed in part against such inconsistency, it is not directed against naturalism as such—I have attempted here to consider the issue purely as a logician, and to suggest to both sides how their positions may be freed from logical faults.

There are, of course, other controversies in moral philosophy in which those on one side or the other, and usually on both, have employed inconclusive arguments, or have fallen into inconsistencies. But this particular controversy has a special interest for the logician, for the following reason: Aristotle divides the possible subjects of inquiry and dispute into three broad sorts—'natural', 'ethical', and 'logical'.[1] Ethical naturalism may be broadly described as the view that 'ethical' propositions and inquiries are in the end just a sub-species of 'natural' ones. But we shall find that both those who assert this and those who deny it frequently end up by identifying ethical propositions with logical ones. And this, of course, imposes upon the logician the responsibility of showing that it is not possible to solve the difficulties of either side in this way.

Having thus confined my field, I have said nothing here, except incidentally in my fourth study, about such matters as the relation between the 'rightness' of actions and the 'goodness' of dispositions or states of affairs, or about that between 'prima facie duties' or 'obligations', which may in given situations be overridden by other 'obligations', and 'actual duties'. Most of the time I have not even troubled to distinguish these concepts, not because I do not consider it important to do so in the proper place, but because they all fall within the 'ethical' sphere, and it is with the relation between that sphere as a whole and the 'natural' and the 'logical' ones that I am here concerned.

I have attempted, nevertheless, to write not so much for the professional logician as for the general student of moral philosophy. I have presumed at one or two points in my second and third studies some memory of what a syllogism is, and what parts it has; but in general I have introduced no

[1] *Topics*, 105^{b}19-29.

logical technicalities without explaining them. The logic which I have employed, and have described others as employing, is for the most part just what used to be called the 'common' logic—the traditional formal logic which has come to us from Aristotle, which was popularized last century by Archbishop Whately, and which has found its most finished modern expression in the *Studies and Exercises in Formal Logic* of Dr. J. N. Keynes. (Whately seems to me to be at present underestimated both as a logician and as a moralist; and in my ninth study I have mentioned one of his own applications of his logical skill to ethical matters; as I have mentioned one of Dr. Keynes's in my fourth.) I have also, particularly in my first study, made use of the *System of Logic* of John Stuart Mill, though not of the 'inductive' portion of it, the importance of which I think both he and many others have overrated, but of the account in his first book of the nature of meaning and definition. And his description of his subject as 'common ground on which the partisans of Hartley and of Reid, of Locke and of Kant, may meet and join hands'[1] is in accord with my own conception of the function of logic in ethical argumentation. At one or two points only, in my fifth and sixth studies, I have had to draw weapons from the larger logical armoury with which the present age has been furnished by Lord Russell and the late Professor Whitehead; but here I have put matters in my own way, and have striven not to be unnecessarily technical.

Such a work as this is not, of course, the place in which to expound a logical system, old or new. The 'logic of ethics' is not a special kind of logic, nor a special branch of logic, but an application of it; and my approach has been largely historical. The nature and possibilities of argument are best studied in arguments that have actually occurred, particularly ones between men who could argue well. I have paid particular attention to the work of the classical English and Scottish

---

[1] Introduction, § 7.

moral philosophers of the eighteenth century, and looked at one or two of my own contemporaries in their light. Although a great deal has been written in recent years about the eighteenth-century moralists (my third study in particular is just a retelling, in my own way and for my own purposes, of a tale that has been told before by an unbroken chain of historians from Dugald Stewart to Dr. D. Daiches Raphael), I doubt whether even yet their relevance to present-day ethical thinking has been fully brought home. I am inclined to think that almost all that can be said, from a purely logical point of view, on the issue between naturalism and anti-naturalism, has already been said in two quite brief sections in Hume's *Treatise of Human Nature* (II. iii. 3, and III. i. 1) and in one quite brief chapter in Reid's *Essays on the Active Powers* (v. vii). At all events, a thorough mastery of these three items would provide anyone with a very complete set of tools for cutting away the thick growths of sophistry which seem in all periods to thrive on the soil of Moral Philosophy. And the 'neutrality' of Logic, at which I have earlier hinted, is well illustrated by the fact that these two writers were, ethically, in opposite camps.

The exposure of fallacious ethical arguments is, however, a task which it seems to be necessary to perform anew in every age. It is something like housekeeping, or lawn-mowing, or shaving. And if I have shown here and there that certain modern writers are not as original as they are sometimes taken to be, I do not wish to be misunderstood as suggesting that their repetitions and restatements of old arguments have no worth or necessity. The unoriginality of Professor Moore, for example, on which I have laid some stress in the following pages, and particularly in my ninth study, does not alter the fact that he has done more than any other single individual to promote clear thinking on ethical subjects in the present century.

It needs also to be said that the 'logic of ethics' owes much to those who have put forward the fallacious arguments which it is its business to expose; and particularly to those who have put them forward in subtle and persuasive forms, and whose language has at the same time been sufficiently precise for their logical errors to be identifiable. For they have not only provided the practising logician with employment, but in so doing have illuminated logical theory. By their inconsistencies they give us fuller insight into what it means *not* to be inconsistent. Even when we know beforehand that some system must be fallacious—that what it sets out to do, simply cannot be done—we learn something in the effort to discover just where the fallacy lies. Of those who have performed this negative service for the logic of ethics, the two who seem to me to be most deserving of our gratitude are William Wollaston and Adam Smith. I should like to add to these names that of my teacher, Professor J. N. Findlay; though I should not like it to be thought that my debt to Professor Findlay is exhausted in his having provided me with something to criticize. I owe to his teaching, directly or indirectly, almost all that I know of either Logic or Ethics; and if I criticize him here, it is only by developing lines of thought into which he himself initiated me.

I

THE NATURALISTIC FALLACY:
THE LOGIC OF ITS REFUTATION

IF there is any contribution to moral philosophy which is more likely than any other to become permanently associated with the name of Professor G. E. Moore, it is the identification and refutation, in his *Principia Ethica*,[1] of what he calls the 'naturalistic fallacy'. I propose now to explain what it is to which Professor Moore gives this name, and what he considers to be involved in its fallaciousness; and I shall offer reasons for regarding his argument, not as disproving ethical naturalism itself, but as exposing an inconsistency into which some naturalists have fallen.

What Professor Moore means by the 'naturalistic fallacy' is the assumption that because some quality or combination of qualities invariably and necessarily accompanies the quality of goodness, or is invariably and necessarily accompanied by it, or both, this quality or combination of qualities is *identical* with goodness. If, for example, it is believed that whatever is pleasant is and must be good, or that whatever is good is and must be pleasant, or both, it is committing the naturalistic fallacy to infer from this that goodness and pleasantness are one and the same quality. The naturalistic fallacy is the assumption that because the words 'good' and, say, 'pleasant' necessarily describe the same objects, they must attribute the same quality to them. We might, with Mill, call the objects to which a term is applicable the denotation of the term, and the characteristics which an object must have for the term to be applicable to it, the connotation of the term.[2] What the man who commits the naturalistic fallacy

[1] pp. 6–17.
[2] J. S. Mill, *System of Logic*, I. ii. 5. The importance of Mill's distinction in the interpretation of Professor Moore's account of the

B

fails to realize is that 'good' and some other adjective may denote or be applicable to the same things, and yet not connote the same quality, i.e. describe the things in the same way. The difference between identity of denotation and identity of connotation may be brought out, as Professor Moore shows, by the following simple consideration: If the word 'good' and, say, the word 'pleasant' apply to the same things, but do not attribute the same quality to them, then to say that what is pleasant is good, or that what is good is pleasant, is to make a significant statement, however obvious its truth may appear to many people. But if the word 'good' and the word 'pleasant' not merely have the same application but the same connotation or 'meaning'—if, that is to say, the quality of pleasantness is identical with the quality of goodness—then to say that what is good is pleasant, or that what is pleasant is good, is to utter an empty tautology, or, as Mill would call it,[1] a 'merely verbal' proposition; for both statements are on this supposition merely ways of saying that what is pleasant is pleasant.

From this consideration Professor Moore attempts to show that the term 'good' is incapable of definition. By 'definition' he means the exhibition of a quality referred to by some term as a combination of simpler qualities. And he argues that if we take any such combination of relatively simple qualities (such as the combination 'being what we desire to desire'), the statement that what possesses this combination of qualities is good (e.g. the statement that what we desire to desire is good) will always be found on careful inspection to be a significant statement and not a mere truism (like 'What we desire to desire, we desire to desire'). But this is not all that he claims to be able to show by this method. We may use

naturalistic fallacy is rightly emphasized in Dr. D. Daiches Raphael's *The Moral Sense*, pp. 111–14; though on p. 113 Dr. Raphael attributes to certain modern mathematicians a confusion in regard to this point, of which I do not think they are really guilty.   [1] *System of Logic*, I. vi.

it, he thinks, to show that goodness is not only simple, i.e. incapable of analysis into simpler parts, but unique. For even if we take a *simple* quality, such as pleasantness, we can always see that it is significant, and not a mere truism, to assert that what possesses this quality is good. (Despite his definition of 'definition', as analysis, he slips readily into calling 'Good means pleasant' a 'definition' too.)

This latter contention of Professor Moore's is exceedingly difficult to state with any precision. It plainly does not apply to the quality of goodness itself—it *is* a truism to assert that what is good is good. Nor does it apply to the quality of goodness itself when it is merely given another name, such as 'value' (which is often used as synonymous with 'goodness' by Professor Moore, as well as by many other writers). Yet if we merely say that goodness is not identical with any other quality, this is itself a truism—it merely tells us that goodness is not identical with any quality, simple or complex, with which it is not identical. It is a little ominous that Professor Moore quotes on his title-page the sentence from Bishop Butler, 'Everything is what it is, and not another thing'. For who would deny this? Even the man who identifies goodness with pleasantness, i.e. who regards 'good' as a mere synonym of 'pleasant', would not deny that it is in this sense 'unique'. For pleasantness also 'is what it is, and not another thing'; and to say that goodness is pleasantness is not, on such a view, to deny that it is what it is, or to affirm that it is another thing—it is merely to deny that pleasantness is 'another thing'.

Professor Moore's real aim, of course, is to show that goodness is not identical with any 'natural' quality. This is why he calls the kind of identification which he is opposing the 'naturalistic' fallacy. But what does he mean by a 'natural' quality? He attempts an answer to this in the *Principia*, but now says that the answer there given is 'utterly silly and preposterous',[1] as indeed it is (there is no need to reproduce

[1] *The Philosophy of G. E. Moore*, p. 582.

it here). And at times it looks very much as if what he means by a 'natural' quality is simply any quality other than goodness or badness, or at all events other than goodness, badness, rightness, wrongness, and obligatoriness (if the last three are taken to be distinct from goodness and badness and from one another—which, in the *Principia Ethica*, they are not), and compounds containing these. But if this is what he means, are we not back where we were?—are we not still left with the truism that 'Everything is what it is, and not another thing'?

It is worth examining this sentence in its original context. Butler's argument in the paragraph from which it is taken[1] is directed against people who were putting it about that it can never be to any man's interest to be virtuous, since disinterestedness is of the essence of virtue. Mandeville, holding that nothing is virtuous but 'self-denial', went so far as to say that virtue was not only not in a man's own interests but generally not in anyone else's either, so that 'private vices' were 'public benefits'. So Butler sets out to show that virtue and disinterestedness are not the same thing (though virtue and self-interest are not the same thing either).

'Virtue and interest, are not to be opposed, but only to be distinguished from each other; in the same way as virtue and any other particular affection, love of arts, suppose, are to be distinguished. Everything is what it is, and not another thing. The goodness or badness of actions does not arise from hence, that the epithet, interested or disinterested, may be applied to them, any more than that any other indifferent epithet, suppose inquisitive or jealous, may or may not be applied to them; not from their being attended with present or future pleasure or pain; but from their being what they are; namely, what becomes such creatures as we are, what the state of the case requires, or the contrary.'

Butler is not, I think, denying that the moral quality of an

---

[1] *Sermons on Human Nature*, Preface, par. 39.

act is determined by its other qualities—he is not denying, for example, that in a given situation a certain intensity of jealousy is always wrong, i.e. 'unbecoming' to 'such creatures as we are'. But he is denying that anything of this sort—expressing jealousy of such-and-such an intensity in such-and-such a situation—is what we *mean* by calling an act good or bad. Its goodness or badness is its 'moral appropriateness' to our nature and our situation. That is, its goodness or badness is its goodness or badness; it is its 'being what it is', good or bad as the case may be. Goodness or badness cannot be identified with any 'indifferent' epithets.

But what kind of epithet is that? If we take 'indifferent' to mean merely 'non-moral'—i.e. if an 'indifferent' epithet is any one that does not mean the same as 'good' or 'bad'—is not Butler's argument open to the same objection as Professor Moore's? Certainly goodness and badness are not to be identified with any qualities that are other than goodness and badness; but how does this forbid us to identify goodness with disinterestedness? Does not the identification of goodness with disinterestedness merely remove the latter from the class of 'indifferent' epithets, i.e. from the class of the 'other things' which goodness is not (just as, on Butler's own view, what we have called 'moral appropriateness' is something that goodness is, 'and not another thing')?

I think we must take it that what Butler means by 'indifference', and Professor Moore by 'naturalness', is something more than mere non-identity with goodness or badness. Their view seems to be that all qualities other than goodness and badness have something positive in common—something which is so near to universal that we do not notice it until we compare the qualities marked by it with goodness and badness; and then it is intuitively evident. When we compare such qualities as goodness and badness with such qualities as pleasantness, pinkness, everlastingness—to take a quite random selection—we see that the former and the latter are not only individually non-identical, as pleasantness and pink-ness are, but fall into two quite different categories or 'realms', namely, those which we sometimes call the realm of value (or of duty) and the realm of fact. These terms are not perhaps quite fortunately chosen, since it may be held—it is held by Professor Moore, for example, and was by Butler—that to say that something is our duty, or possesses value, is to state a fact, albeit of a very peculiar kind. (We shall see in the sixth and seventh studies that there are some writers who deny this; but such a denial seems to amount to saying that there is really only one realm—the 'natural' one—and this is not the position which we are at present trying to formu-late.) But however we describe these two 'realms', their existence and distinctness is what seems to be referred to in Professor Moore's distinction between ethical predicates and all 'natural' ones, as it is in the old distinction betweeen the 'moral' perfections of the Deity and His 'natural' ones (omni-potence, omniscience, eternity, &c.), and in Aristotle's distinc-tion between the 'ethical', the 'natural', and the 'logical' fields of inquiry. And Aristotle notes that 'the nature of each of the aforesaid kinds of proposition is not easily rendered in a defini-tion, but we have to try to recognize each of them by means of the familiarity attained through induction, examining them in the light' of certain 'illustrations' given previously—'ethical' questions being illustrated by 'Ought one rather to obey one's parents or the laws, if they disagree?' and 'natural' ones by 'Is the universe eternal or not?'[1] (Aristotle is here using 'induction' to mean, not a process of reason-ing, but the examining of instances until their common quality 'dawns' upon one—his appeal is to intuition.) But such an intuitively perceived difference between 'moral' qualities and all others plainly goes far beyond anything that can be proved from the principle that 'Everything is what it is and not another thing', since this principle would

[1] *Topics*, 105^{b}21–9.

still apply within a single 'natural' realm even if there were no other.[1]

Professor Moore's appeal to this truism, and the little dialectical device which he bases upon it, are not, however, entirely pointless. For there *are* occasions when men implicitly deny logical truisms, and need to be reminded of them; namely, when they are inconsistent. It is not against the naturalist as such, but the inconsistent naturalist, the man who tries to 'have it both ways', that Professor Moore's type of argument is really effective and important. And such people are not uncommon. Professor Moore himself mentions them—the people who begin by laying it down as a truth of primary importance, perhaps even as something rather revolutionary, that nothing is good but pleasure, or that nothing is good but what promotes biological survival, and who, when asked why they are so certain of this, reply that 'that is the very meaning of the word'. To such people it is certainly legitimate and necessary to reply that if pleasantness, or the promotion of survival, is what 'goodness' *means*, then the fact that only pleasure is good, or that only what promotes survival is good, is hardly worth shouting from the house-tops, since nobody in his senses ever denied that what is pleasant, and only what is pleasant, is pleasant, or that what promotes survival, and only what promotes survival, promotes survival. What these people would plainly like to hold is that goodness is both identical with pleasantness and not identical with it; and, of course, it cannot be done. They want to regard 'What is pleasant is good' as a significant assertion; and it can only be so if the pleasantness of what is pleasant is one thing, and its goodness another. On the other hand they want to make it logically impossible to contradict this assertion—they want to treat the opposing assertion that what is pleasant may not be good as not merely false but logically

[1] This point is elaborated in an article on 'The Naturalistic Fallacy', by W. K. Frankena, in *Mind*, 1939, pp. 472 ff.

absurd—and this can only be done if pleasantness and goodness are taken to be identical. To represent an opponent's
position in such a way as to make it not only false but self-
contradictory is a dialectical triumph which can never be
obtained without being duly paid for; and the price is the
representation of one's position as not only true but a truism.
'If a denial is to have any value as a statement of matter of
fact', as Dr. J. N. Keynes says,[1] then what it denies 'must be
consistent with the meaning of the terms employed. . . . The
denial of a contradiction in terms . . . yields merely what is
tautologous and practically useless.'

It is sometimes pointed out by naturalists that there is
never more than one ethical statement which is rendered
trivial by a naturalistic definition of 'good'. If, for example,
we use 'good' as synonymous with 'conducive to biological
survival', then, while it is a truism to say that what is conducive
to biological survival is 'good' in this sense, it is not a truism
to say that pleasure is, since it is not a truism to say that
pleasure is conducive to survival. We shall find shortly that
there is a point at which this consideration is important; but
if Professor Moore's argument is regarded as a criticism of
the attempt to deduce significant assertions from definitions,
this answer to it is irrelevant, since the statement which the
definition makes trivial is always precisely the one which it is
put forward to 'prove', in a sense in which it is not trivial but
significant. A man who has defined 'good' as 'conducive to
biological survival', with the express purpose of establishing
it as an ethical principle of primary importance that only
what conduces to survival is good, will not be greatly cheered
by the consideration that it is 'only' this principle which the
definition renders insignificant.

Confronted with Professor Moore's argument, an inconsistent ethical naturalist has two courses open to him. He may
clear himself of inconsistency, on the one hand, by abandon-

[1] *Formal Logic*, pp. 119–20.

ing his naturalism—he may continue to insist that only pleasure, or conduciveness to survival, or whatever it may be, is good, but may preserve the significance of this assertion by sacrificing its certainty, admitting that its denial, though still in his opinion false, is not self-contradictory. Professor Moore writes as if this is what any naturalist who really grasps his argument will do—he seems to consider his argument a *refutation* of naturalism. But a naturalist can preserve his naturalism if he wants to, even in the face of Professor Moore's argument—he can do so by admitting that the assertion that, say, pleasure and nothing but pleasure is good, *is* for him a mere truism; and that if Ethics be the attempt to determine what is in fact good, then the statement that what is pleasant is good is not, strictly speaking, an ethical statement, but only a way of indicating just what study is to go under the name of 'Ethics'—the study of what is actually pleasant, without any pretence of maintaining that pleasure has any 'goodness' beyond its pleasantness. He might add at the same time that he is not only not going to discuss goodness as a 'non-natural' quality, but that in his belief there is no such quality, and that this is worth shouting from the house-tops, as it liberates us from a transcendental notion which has haunted us too long. (He might say that this is what he really means by the assertion that 'Nothing is good but pleasure' —he means, not that what is pleasant alone possesses some other quality called 'goodness', but that there are no qualities beyond 'natural' ones such as pleasantness to which the word 'goodness' could be applied.) Indeed, he is bound to say something of this sort if he is to justify his appropriation of the word 'good' for the purpose to which he puts it. And such a man, it seems to me, should be prepared to state his position in an alternative way, namely, as a denial that there *is* such a study as Ethics—he should be prepared, for the sake of clarity, and to further the mental 'liberation' in which he is primarily interested, to call his inquiry into the sources of pleasure, not Ethics, but some such name as 'Hedonics'; or if he defines goodness as 'conduciveness to survival', to call his substitute for Ethics 'Biological Strategy'.

But how—as Mr. E. F. Carritt pertinently asks[1]—can we be 'liberated' from a notion which we cannot ever have had? For how can we have had a 'transcendental' notion of goodness if the word which is alleged to have called it up is also alleged to have no meaning, or none beyond ones which are not 'transcendental' at all? Even this question it is not beyond the power of a consistent naturalist to answer.

'A name', as J. S. Mill points out, 'is not imposed at once and by previous purpose upon a *class* of objects, but is first applied to one thing, and then extended by a series of transitions to another. By this process . . . a name not unfrequently passes by successive links of resemblance from one object to another, until it becomes applied to things having nothing in common with the first things to which the name was given; which, however, do not, for that reason, drop the name; so that it at last denotes a confused huddle of objects, having nothing whatever in common; and connotes nothing, not even a vague and general resemblance. When a name has fallen into this state, . . . it has become unfit for the purposes either of thought or of the communication of thought; and can only be made serviceable by stripping it of some part of its multifarious denotation, and confining it to objects possessed of some attributes in common, which it may be made to connote.'[2]

And this, a naturalist may say, is precisely what has happened with the word 'good', and what needs to be done about it. At present, when we call a thing good we may mean that it is pleasant, or that it is commanded by someone, or that it is customary, or that it promotes survival, or any one of a number of things; and because we use the same term to connote all these characteristics, we think there must be some other single characteristic which they all entail; but in

[1] *Ethical and Political Thinking*, pp. 33–4.
[2] *System of Logic*, I. viii. 7; see also IV. iv. 5, v. 2.

fact there is not. When it is said that being good means promoting survival, we are dissatisfied; we feel that it is still significant to say that promoting survival is good; and the same thing happens with every identification that is suggested; but this is just because, in each case, the other meanings are still hovering in our minds—to say that promoting survival is good is significant because it means that to promote survival is what we desire; to say that what we desire is good is significant because it means that what we desire promotes survival; and so on. Once we realize this, we may either recommend and adopt a more consistent usage; or we may leave the word with its present 'flexibility', but with the misleading suggestions of that flexibility removed. The naturalist who proposes some unambiguous definition is taking the first course.[1]

This way of dealing with words like 'good' is characteristic of the 'therapeutic positivism' developed at Cambridge in the past few decades under the influence of Professor Wittgenstein. While this is unquestionably a useful philosophical technique, there are obvious limits to its applicability. For it is plain that in some cases in which diverse objects are called by a common name there *is* a common characteristic on account of which the name is given to them all. We need some principle enabling us to decide when such a common characteristic exists and when it does not; and what principle we use for this purpose will depend upon our general philosophical position. Analyses of the sort just given cannot therefore replace philosophical inquiry, as 'therapeutic positivists' seem at times to think they can, but both aid it and depend upon it. If we have other reasons for regarding the distinction between the 'natural' and the 'moral' realms as an illusory one, then tricks of language may explain how the

---

[1] For an answer to Professor Moore along these general lines see a dialogue by E. and M. Clark entitled 'What is Goodness?' in the *Australasian Journal of Psychology and Philosophy*, 1941.

illusion has come about; but it may still, as a matter of fact, be real.

It remains true, however, that a naturalist *can* extricate himself from Professor Moore's trap if he is bold enough and tough enough. And in imagining that in his refutation of what he calls the 'naturalistic fallacy' he has refuted naturalism, Professor Moore has himself fallen into a fallacy not unlike it. For if Professor Moore's own non-naturalism is a significant belief, then it must be possible to formulate the naturalism which it contradicts in a significant way; and if naturalism itself, and not merely the inadvertent combination of naturalism with something inconsistent with it, is senseless, then the denial of it is trivial. A significant non-naturalism, in other words, must comprise more than mere freedom from the 'naturalistic fallacy'.

II

THE AUTONOMY OF ETHICS: (1) CUDWORTH

THE same broad type of moral philosophy as Professor Moore has taught at Cambridge in our own time was also taught there in the seventeenth century by that difficult but rewarding writer Ralph Cudworth. Cudworth is mentioned by Rashdall[1] as anticipating Professor Moore's opinion that 'good is indefinable'; and, as we shall see shortly, he defended this opinion by the same bad argument. But like Professor Moore he also had a good argument against ethical naturalists who could not be quite consistent; and though it was not quite the same argument as Professor Moore's, it is equally worthy of our attention, and we shall accordingly study it, indicating in later studies how it was developed by later and clearer writers.

The inconsistent ethical naturalism which Cudworth criticized took the form of an identification of goodness or rightness (as I have already indicated, it is not necessary for my present purpose to distinguish sharply between these) with obedience to someone's will—the civil sovereign's or God's—coupled with an insistence, as if it were an insistence on something of the first importance, that to obey this person is good or right, and to disobey him bad or wrong—an insistence, in short, that we have in some significant sense a duty to obey him. Hobbes, in particular, sometimes spoke in this way about the civil ruler, and Descartes and various theologians about God. Against all attempts to make goodness thus completely dependent on a superior's will, Cudworth argues that

'Moral good and evil . . . cannot possibly be arbitrary things, made by will without nature; because it is universally true, that things are what they are, not by will but by nature. As for ex-

[1] *The Theory of Good and Evil*, vol. i, p. 136.

ample, things are white by whiteness, and black by blackness, triangular by triangularity, and round by rotundity, like by likeness, and equal by equality, that is, by such certain natures of their own. Neither can Omnipotence itself (to speak with reverence) by mere will make a thing white or black without whiteness or blackness. . . . Or . . . to instance in things relative only; omnipotent will cannot make things like or equal one to another, without the natures of likeness or equality. The reason whereof is plain, because all these things imply a manifest contradiction; that things should be what they are not. Now things may as well be made white or black by mere will, without whiteness or blackness, equal and unequal, without equality and inequality, as morally good and evil, just and unjust, honest and dishonest, debita and illicita, by mere will, without any nature of goodness, justice, honesty. . . . And since a thing cannot be made any thing by mere will without a being or nature, every thing must be necessarily and immutably determined by its own nature, and the nature of things be that which it is, and nothing else. For though the will and power of God have an absolute, infinite and unlimited command upon the existences of all created things to make them to be, or not to be at pleasure; yet when things exist, they are what they are, this or that, absolutely or relatively, not by will or arbitrary command, but by the necessity of their own nature. There is no such thing as an arbitrarious essence, mode or relation, that may be made indifferently any thing at pleasure; for an arbitrarious essence is a being without a nature, a contradiction, and therefore a nonentity. Wherefore the natures of justice and injustice cannot be arbitrarious things, that may be applicable by will indifferently to any actions or dispositions whatsoever.'[1]

This is not easy reading, but Cudworth's point appears to be that any quality of an object is what it is—whiteness, say, is whiteness—wherever it may be found; that what sort of a thing anything is depends entirely on its possessing the characteristic quality of that sort of thing; that we cannot, God Himself cannot, cause a thing to *be* of a certain sort

---

[1] *Treatise concerning Eternal and Immutable Morality*, I. ii. 1, 2; Selby-Bigge, *British Moralists*, §§ 813–15.

without its having the quality in question; that God may at His pleasure cause these qualities or 'natures' to be or cease to be exemplified in objects, but that He cannot cause any quality itself to be anything but what it is. And so, though goodness and badness may be and cease to be exemplified in particular acts, goodness can never be anything but goodness, and badness can never be anything but badness, nor can a thing be good without goodness or bad without badness.

But what has all this to do with the refutation of Hobbes and Descartes? Is not obedience also obedience wherever it may be found? Is it not also a 'nature' which acts may come to possess and cease to possess; and are not obedient acts what they are by obedience, and disobedient ones by dis-obedience? We must surely say with Tulloch that Cudworth 'is here merely stating an identical proposition—that what is moral is moral—that a thing cannot be moral and with-out morality—a proposition which no one would deny. But such a proposition throws no light on the question, why a thing is moral and not immoral?'[1] Obedience is, indeed, strictly speaking, not a quality of an action, but a relation of it to a command; and Mr. J. A. Passmore has defended Cud-worth against Tulloch's charge of triviality on the ground that his main point is that the morality of an act lies in its 'character' or qualities.[2] But if this is what Cudworth is really setting out to prove, his appeal to the principles of identity and contradiction does not take him a single step towards proving it, particularly since he himself explicitly applies these principles to relations as well as qualities. 'Things are what they are, *absolutely or relatively*.' Things are equal, for example, only if the relation of equality—which, like the quality of whiteness, is what it is wherever it may be found—holds between them. And an act is obedient only if

---

[1] *Rational Theology in the Nineteenth Century*, p. 285.
[2] 'The Moral Philosophy of Cudworth', *Australasian Journal of Psychology and Philosophy*, 1942, p. 172.

the relation of obedience holds between it and a command. Certainly acts of the same sort, i.e. with the same qualities, may be obedient and disobedient in relation to different commands; but so may things of the same sort be equal and unequal to different things; and while God can make, say, a kind act obedient by commanding kindness, and an unkind one by commanding unkindness, He cannot make a disobedient act obedient in any way at all. He might, indeed, command that He be disobeyed, and some writers of Cudworth's period brought up just this point against this sort of theory;[1] but I think a modern logician would say that such a 'command' is not a command at all, just as he would say that 'What I am now saying is false' is not a genuine proposition. He would say this, at least, if the command in question were understood as God's command to disobey all His commands, including itself. If it is understood simply as a command abrogating all other commands, or all other commands except one abrogating it, and any ones subsequent to that, then it presents no difficulty; for it is not then disobedience as such which is being commanded—it is not, in Cudworth's language, acts which have the 'nature' of disobedience which are being made obedient—it is just that the commands to which we may be obedient or disobedient are being altered.

Since, then, obedience and disobedience are 'natures' as much as all other qualities and relations are, why should they not be the 'natures' referred to by the terms 'goodness' and badness'? How has Cudworth's argument shown that there are any other 'natures' to which they could refer? Why may it not be that—as he suggests in a brief parenthesis his opponents might hold—'moral good and evil, just and unjust,

[1] e.g. Turretinus, *Institutio Theologiae Elencticae*, Loc. III, Q. xviii, § vi: 'Si voluntas Dei esset prima regula justitiae etiam ab intrinseco, ut nihil esset bonum et justum nisi quia Deus vult; . . . posset esse author et approbator inobedientiae hominis, posset enim illi mandare ne sibi quodcunque praecipienti aut vetanti obediat.'

honest and dishonest' are 'mere names without any signification, or names for nothing else, but willed and commanded'?

Mr. Passmore points out[1] that Cudworth did not take this
last possibility seriously as what Hobbes and Descartes might
be principally concerned to maintain; and he was on surer
ground when he observed that, if we take seriously their other
view that the term 'obligation' has a distinct meaning, and
that we have an obligation to obey our civil rulers, or God,
then this obligation itself cannot be 'created out of nothing'
by their will and command. Even in cases—and Cudworth
admits that there are such cases—where a command makes
something obligatory which was not so before,

'mere will doth not make the thing commanded just or debitum,
"obligatory", or beget and create any obligation to obedience.
Therefore it is observable that laws and commands do not run
thus, to will that this or that thing shall become justum or inju-
stum, debitum or illicitum, "just or unjust, obligatory or unlawful";
or that man shall be obliged or bound to obey; but only to require
that something be done or not done, or otherwise to menace
punishment to the transgressors thereof. For it was never heard
of, that any one founded all his authority of commanding others,
and others obligation or duty to obey his commands, in a law of
his own making, that men should be required, obliged, or bound
to obey him. Wherefore since the thing willed in all laws is not
that men should be bound or obliged to obey; this thing cannot
be the product of the mere will of the commander, but it must
proceed from something else; namely, the right or authority of
the commander, which is founded in natural justice and equity,
and an antecedent obligation to obedience in the subjects; which
things are not made by laws, but presupposed before all laws to
make them valid. And if it should be imagined, that any one
should make a positive law to require that others should be
obliged, or bound to obey him, every one would think such a law
ridiculous and absurd; for if they were obliged before, then this
law would be in vain, and to no purpose; and if they were not

[1] Op. cit., p. 173.

before obliged, then they could not be obliged by any positive law, because they were not previously bound to obey such a person's commands; so that obligation to obey all positive laws is older than all laws, and previous or antecedent to them. . . . And if this were not morally good and just in its own nature before any positive command of God, that God should be obeyed of his creatures, the bare will of God himself could not beget an obligation upon any to do what he willed and commanded.'[1]

It is this passage, I think, which Adam Smith is paraphrasing when he writes;

'Law, it was justly observed by Dr. Cudworth, could not be the original source of these distinctions'—i.e. the distinctions between right and wrong, laudable and blameable, virtuous and vicious—'since, upon the supposition of such a law, it must either be right to obey it and wrong to disobey it, or indifferent whether we obeyed it or disobeyed it. That law which it was indifferent whether we obeyed or disobeyed, could not, it was evident, be the source of those distinctions; neither could that which it was right to obey and wrong to disobey, since this still supposed the antecedent notions or ideas of right and wrong, and that obedience to the law was conformable to the idea of right, and disobedience to that of wrong.'[2]

This is not quite Professor Moore's point that if obligatoriness is a character which may be significantly predicated of some person's commands, then it cannot just *mean* being commanded by that person; though Smith's paraphrase comes somewhat closer to this than Cudworth's original. The point is rather that it is impossible to deduce an ethical conclusion from entirely non-ethical premisses. We cannot infer 'We ought to do X' from, for example, 'God commands us to do X', unless this is supplemented by the ethical premiss,

[1] Op. cit. I. ii. 3; Selby-Bigge, § 816.
[2] *Theory of Moral Sentiments*, Part VII, Sect. III. ch. ii. The reference given by Smith is to Cudworth's 'Immutable Morality, I. i'; but in I. i. there is no such argument, but only a preliminary account of the views which he is to attack in I. ii.

'We ought to do what God commands'; and it is quite useless to offer instead of this some additional non-ethical premiss, such as 'God commands us to obey His commands'. That this is Cudworth's main contention is plain from the paragraph following the one last quoted, in which he says:

'That common distinction betwixt things, φύσει and θέσει, "things naturally and positively good and evil", or (as others express it) betwixt things that are therefore commanded because they are good and just, and things that are therefore good and just, because they are commanded, stands in need of a right explication, that we be not led into a mistake thereby, as if the obligation to do those thetical and positive things did arise wholly from will without nature. . . . The difference of these things lies wholly in this, That there are some things which the intellectual nature'—i.e. their character as perceived by the intellect—'obligeth to per se, "of itself", and directly, absolutely and perpetually, and these things are called "naturally good and evil"; other things there are which the same intellectual nature obligeth to by accident only, and hypothetically, upon condition of some voluntary action either of our own or some other person's, by means whereof those things which were in their own nature indifferent, falling under something that is absolutely good or evil, and thereby acquiring a new relation to the intellectual nature, do for the time become debita or illicita, "such things as ought to be done or omitted", being made such not by will but by nature. As for example, to keep faith and perform covenants, is that which natural justice obligeth to absolutely; therefore, ex hypothesi, "upon the supposition" that any one maketh a promise, which is a voluntary act of his own, to do something which he was not before obliged to by natural justice, upon the intervention of this voluntary act of his own, that indifferent thing promised falling now under something absolutely good, and becoming the matter of promise and covenant, standeth for the present in a new relation to the rational nature of the promiser, and becometh for the time the thing which ought to be done by him, or which he is obliged to do. . . . In like manner natural justice, that is, the rational or intellectual nature, obligeth not only to obey God, but also civil powers, that have lawful authority of commanding, and to observe political order amongst men; and therefore if God or civil powers command any thing to be done that is not unlawful in itself, upon the intervention of this voluntary act of theirs, those things that were before indifferent, become by accident for the time debita, "obligatory", such things as ought to be done by us, not for their own sakes, but for the sake of that which natural justice absolutely obligeth to.'[1]

To do X is good by accident when it 'falls under' a promise, to keep which is good by nature, or a command, to obey which is good by nature. ('Falling under' is the literal translation of *accidens*.) To anyone acquainted with the Aristotelian logic, this use of the phrase 'falling under' immediately suggests the minor premiss of a syllogism; and it is fairly clear that at the back of Cudworth's mind were the two syllogisms:

> To keep a promise is good;
> To do X is to keep a promise;
> Therefore, To do X is good;

and

> To obey A is good;
> To do X is to obey A;
> Therefore, To do X is good.

Cudworth also says that the 'moral goodness, justice and virtue' involved in obeying lawful commands, in matters in themselves indifferent, 'consisteth not in the materiality of the actions themselves, but in that formality of yielding obedience to the commands of lawful authority in them'. Similarly the virtue of keeping a promise or contract in matters indifferent 'consisteth not in the materiality of the action promised, but in the formality of keeping faith and performing covenants'.[2] He means that there are only a certain fixed number of characteristics which cannot be

---

[1] Op. cit. I. ii. 4; Selby-Bigge, § 817.
[2] Op. cit. I. ii. 5; Selby-Bigge, § 820.

present in actions without goodness being present in them too, and that even a promise or a lawful command to do an act of the character X cannot cause the character X to be one of these 'good-making' characters if it was not so before; it can only cause particular acts of the character X to have the additional character of being the fulfilment of a promise or the meeting of a lawful command, which additional character is and always was a 'good-making' one. Even this very quali-fied admission that commands and promises may give an 'accidental' goodness to what is neither good nor bad apart from them is regarded by Mr. Passmore as a concession to Hobbes and Descartes which is inconsistent with Cudworth's general position;[1] but I think this is only because Mr. Pass-more attaches more importance to the difference between qualities and relations than Cudworth himself does, and fails to notice that relational characters are included among those which Cudworth calls 'natures'.

Cudworth's classification of promises and contracts along with commands as acts of will which cannot give rise to obligations apart from a more fundamental obligation to act in accordance with them is directed against an attempt by Hobbes to derive all our obligations, not directly from the command of the ruler, but from a supposed agreement with others to obey him. Dealing more specifically with this view elsewhere, Cudworth observes that

'though it be true that if there be natural justice, covenants will oblige; yet, upon the contrary supposition, that there is nothing naturally unjust, this cannot be unjust neither, to break covenants. Covenants, without natural justice, are nothing but mere words and breath, (as indeed these atheistic politicians themselves, agree-ably to their own hypothesis, call them); and therefore can they have no force to oblige.'[2]

Shaftesbury, writing a little later, takes the same line.

''Tis ridiculous to say there is any obligation on man to act

[1] Op. cit., pp. 174 ff.   [2] *Intellectual System of the Universe*, v. v. 24.

sociably or honestly in a formed government, and not in that which is commonly called the state of nature. For, to speak in the fashionable language of our modern philosophy: "Society being founded on a compact, the surrender made of every man's private unlimited right, into the hands of the majority, or such as the majority should appoint, was of free choice, and by a promise." Now the promise itself was made in the state of nature; and . . . he who was free to any villainy before his contract, will and ought to make as free with his contract when he thinks fit. The natural knave has the same reason to be a civil one, and may dispense with his politic capacity as oft as he sees occasion. 'Tis only his word stands in his way. . . . A man is obliged to keep his word. Why? Because he has given his word to keep it. . . . Is not this a notable account of the original of moral justice, and the rise of civil government and allegiance!'[1]

We cannot, in short, infer 'We ought to do X' from 'We have promised to do X', unless we also grant the ethical proposition 'We ought to keep promises', and for this latter, no non-ethical substitutes, such as 'We have promised to keep our promises', will do.

Hobbes himself perceived that he would be open to this line of criticism if he did not state his position carefully; so we sometimes find him admitting that the keeping of agreements, at least of some agreements, is a 'law of nature', i.e. is of its own nature obligatory, independently of commands and agreements. But he attempted to diminish the seriousness of this admission by adding that what he called 'laws of nature' are only so called by courtesy (since a law in the proper sense is simply the command of someone with power to enforce it); what they really are are 'conclusions or theorems' which may be worked out 'concerning what conduceth to the conservation and defence of ourselves'.[2] In that case, as Cudworth observes, what Hobbes and others like him call 'laws of nature' are only 'the laws of their own timorous

---

[1] *An Essay on the Freedom of Wit and Humour*, Part III, Sect. I.
[2] *Leviathan*, ch. 15.

and cowardly complexion; for they, who have courage and generosity in them, . . . would never submit to such sneaking terms of equality and subjection, but venture for dominion; and resolve either to win the saddle or lose the horse'.[1] There is a curious anticipation of Nietzsche here—not that Cudworth was a Nietzschean (the real precursor of Nietzsche in his period, or very shortly after it, was Mandeville); but he saw that if a man was going to be an 'amoralist', then he might well be so constituted as to like the 'war of all against all' which Hobbes thought would be the state of men without government (and which nineteenth-century Darwinians regarded as prevailing in the biological world), so that as far as such a man was concerned, Hobbes's 'theorems' or recipes for living in peace and safety would fall on deaf ears.

Mr. Passmore sees in this part of Cudworth's argument an exposure of Hobbes's inconsistency in asserting 'that to act well *means* to do what is commanded', while at the same time arguing 'that a person who does what is commanded acts well, as if this were not, on his showing, a tautology'[2]—he sees in it, that is, an anticipation of the argument of Professor Moore. But although all these arguments tend to run into one another, what Cudworth says here seems to be an anticipation not so much of Professor Moore as of Mr. Passmore himself, when he points out elsewhere that since the 'laws of nature' as Hobbes understands them simply 'present the means that we will have to adopt if we are to live at peace', they are 'mandatory only on those who wish to do so. In Kantian language, they are hypothetical, or at most assertorial, and not categorical imperatives'; though 'there can be little doubt' that Hobbes wanted to make more of them, and that 'he could not help feeling that anyone who lacked this fear of anarchy, anyone who preferred war to peace, was

[1] Op. cit.
[2] Op. cit., p. 173.

morally reprehensible'.[1] The point is, I think, that if Hobbes is merely offering an explanation of why *some* men (the intelligent lovers of peace) *are* law-abiding, he has neither established nor overthrown any view as to why *all* men *ought* to be so; he has simply changed the subject.

We shall find in our final study that the special argument which has come to be associated with the name of Professor Moore has been used by quite a number of writers before him; but the argument that no ethical conclusion can be inferred from entirely non-ethical premisses is both older and more common. It is, I think, easier for most people to follow; and it compendiously refutes a greater variety of fallacies, including the one that Professor Moore refutes as a special case. For if it is impossible to deduce an ethical proposition from any entirely non-ethical premiss or set of premisses, then it is impossible to deduce one from a definition, since a definition, if it is properly to be called a proposition at all, is not one about obligations, but one about the meaning of words. (At the same time, definitions of 'obligation' and other moral terms look as if they are about obligations, and as if significant propositions about obligations might be deducible from them, and Professor Moore's argument is often necessary as a supplementary measure to destroy this illusion.) And just as a naturalist may make his position consistent by accepting the conclusion to which Professor Moore's argument forces him, so a consistent naturalist may, on the wider issue, agree that ethical conclusions require ethical premisses, and formulate his disagreement with the non-naturalist as a disagreement as to what is to count as an 'ethical premiss'.[2] One sort of consistent naturalist might say, for instance, that 'We probably ought to reverence our parents' ('To reverence our parents is probably good')

[1] 'The Moral Philosophy of Hobbes.' *Australasian Journal of Psychology and Philosophy*, 1941, p. 42.
[2] This point is developed by W. K. Frankena, *Mind*, 1939, pp. 468–9.

follows from 'Reverence for parents is inculcated in the communities which have lasted longest' and 'What is inculcated in the communities which have lasted longest is probably conducive to biological survival', not because ethical conclusions ever follow from non-ethical premisses, but because 'What is inculcated in the communities which have lasted longest is probably conducive to biological survival' is not, on his view, a non-ethical premiss, but a more precise way of saying 'What is inculcated in the communities which have lasted longest is probably good'. There is no answer to this; though the naturalist may be reminded that he has only proved that we probably ought to reverence our parents in the sense that such action is probably conducive to survival— he has provided those interested in survival with a recipe which will probably ensure it; and if he claims to have done more, we have him at once.

III

THE AUTONOMY OF ETHICS:
(2) CLARKE TO REID

THE tendency to fall into fallacious modes of reasoning is rather like an epidemic that breaks out during a war. It strikes one side first, giving a temporary advantage to the other; but it has a way of drifting across the line of battle and infecting those who formerly had the satisfaction of being free from it. This fact is illustrated, even quite dramatically, by the history, after Cudworth, of the fallacious claim to deduce ethical conclusions from non-ethical premisses.

When Cudworth speaks of 'natural' laws, rights, and duties as being presupposed in the morally binding character of 'positive' ones, he is not contrasting the 'natural' realm with the 'moral'. On the contrary, both he and other writers of his period frequently use 'natural' and 'moral' as synonyms; he speaks, for example, of the duty of obeying God both as a 'moral' one and as one founded in 'natural' justice. It is, rather, 'positive' law which is 'natural' in Professor Moore's sense—a fact of nature, whether it be morally good or evil. And what Hobbes calls a 'natural' law, though it is different from 'positive' law, is still a fact of nature in this sense—that is where his usage differs from Cudworth's. Hobbes's 'natural' laws, in fact, are not far removed from what modern scientists would call by the name—they are 'natural tendencies' of men and societies. But Hobbes's usage is not consistent, since he sometimes seems to think he has established a 'natural' duty (in Cudworth's sense) of keeping agreements, when he has at most established a 'natural tendency', at least among wise men, to do so. I doubt whether moral writers are even yet quite free from this confusion. Dr. K. R. Popper, for example, in the chapter on 'Nature and Convention' in

The Open Society and its Enemies, seems sometimes to be opposing the view that there are 'natural' duties, in Cudworth's sense, on the grounds that it is impossible to infer any duties from 'natural tendencies'.

The phrase 'good by nature' has also caused confusion through the conflict between tendencies to identify it, and tendencies not to identify it, with 'good by definition'. I think this double use of 'good by nature'—to mean 'good by definition', and at the same time something more than this—is an instance of the fallacy which Dr. Popper calls 'essentialism'. Here the chief offenders have not been Hobbes and his followers, but Cudworth and his. And through this ambiguity many quite unimpeachably non-naturalistic writers have fallen into the illusion of deducing ethical propositions from non-ethical ones, the indispensable ethical premiss, when attention is drawn to it, being passed off as 'only a definition'. The whole process is sometimes called showing the 'foundations' in nature of our various duties. It might begin with a demonstration of God's existence, followed by a proof that His purpose in making us was that our reason should govern our instincts; and from this it is concluded that our reason *ought* to govern our instincts. The conclusion plainly cannot be drawn unless it is also granted that we 'ought' to accomplish God's purposes for us; but this premiss is thought to be such a 'little one' as to be hardly worth mentioning; for 'after all, it is of the very nature of our relation to our Maker that we ought to obey Him—to say that we ought to obey Him is just to say that He *is* our Maker'. But either this statement is significant or it is not. If we mean by calling God our Maker not only that He has made us but that we ought to obey Him, then that we ought to obey our Maker, i.e. that we ought to obey a Being whom we ought to obey, is plainly true, but hardly to the purpose. If we mean that any Being who stands to us in the *other* relations in which God stands to us, cannot but also be One whom we ought to obey, then this is more than a definition, and is a premiss that requires to be set down; and either its 'foundation' must be shown, or it must be admitted that not all duties can be provided with a 'foundation'. (This confusion of a tautology with a significant proposition, resulting from the identification of a significant proposition with a definition, is like the confusion which Professor Moore calls the 'naturalistic fallacy'; but it is not quite the same, as the tautologies in question arise, not from a naturalistic definition of 'good', but from a non-naturalistic definition of what is said to *be* good. 'Obedient to God' is not said to be 'the very meaning of the word "good"'; but 'having a duty to obey God' is said to be part of what it 'means' to be His creature.)

This is a simplified general scheme rather than an accurate reproduction of the views of any particular writer. (It is based on personal experience of controversy with Thomists more than on anything else.) But there is more than a hint of it in the endless irrelevancies about the laws of identity and contradiction in which Cudworth indulges when he is trying to prove that there must be some things which are good, not because anyone has commanded them, but simply because 'they are what they are'. What Cudworth undoubtedly means to maintain is that there are certain qualities—generosity, loyalty, &c.—of which we can say that whatever acts possess them are thereby determined as possessing another quality, 'goodness'. But this is neither identical with nor deducible from the fact that whatever is good is good. In the early eighteenth century we find Samuel Clarke speaking in the same ambiguous way of an act as being right or fitting because the situation in which it is performed 'is what it is'. Here again it is clear that what Clarke really believes is that situations of certain kinds 'call for' acts of certain kinds, and do so with a self-evidence as clear as that of the propositions of geometry; and this self-evidence leads him to speak sometimes as if to say that a situation of a certain kind 'calls for' a certain kind of action is no more than to say that it is the kind of situation it is. Bishop Butler thought Clarke's approach a little abstract for the majority of men, and it seemed to him that vice could be more effectively attacked as 'a violation or breaking in upon *our own* nature' than as 'contrary to the nature of things';[1] but he is full of the same kind of sophistry. I am thinking now, not of his direct appeal to the dictum that 'Everything is what it is, and not another thing', but of his well-known claim to base the obligation to be virtuous on the 'constitution' of human nature, a claim which he attempts to make good by telling us that it is an essential part of this 'constitution' that our conscience should govern all our other inward urges. If this is not an assertion that a man's conscience always proves itself stronger than anything else in him, and Butler certainly neither believed nor said this, then it is either a tautology or a proposition which is already ethical and not merely about how the human mechanism in fact operates. If 'conscience' means 'that in us which we ought to obey'—and it is not easy to see what else 'conscience' does mean in Butler—then it is a truism that conscience has authority to rule in us, i.e. that we ought to obey it. Or if Butler does mean something other than this by 'conscience', then his assertion that it is part of the 'constitution of human nature' that conscience should rule in us would seem to be a way of saying that a man in whom conscience does not rule is not, properly speaking, a man. But either this means that a 'man' is to be defined as, among other things, a being in whom conscience 'has power as it has authority', in which case nothing of significance can be proved from it (Butler is asking us not to *call* a being who disobeys his conscience a man; that is all); or it means that a man who disobeys his conscience is not an ideal or good man, i.e. that we ought to obey our conscience, and this is so far from being a non-moral 'foundation' of Ethics that it is not

[1] *Sermons on Human Nature*, Preface, par. 12.

merely a moral proposition but—since 'obedient to conscience' is what Butler seems to mean by 'virtuous'—the
precise moral principle which he sets out to prove. On this
last interpretation, his 'proof' amounts to this, that we ought
to obey our conscience because we ought to, or we ought to
obey it because it is our conscience; and while these are not
truisms like 'Our conscience is our conscience' or 'We ought
to do what we ought to', they are not 'proofs' either, but
rather ways of saying that the obligation to obey conscience
cannot be proved.

Ethical rationalism—the belief that the mind may perceive
real and distinctive ethical qualities in actions (Cudworth), or
real and distinctive ethical relations between acts and situations
(Clarke), or between elements in our personality (Butler)—
fell into considerable disrepute in the middle of the eighteenth
century, precisely through its entanglement with this new
form of the illusion that ethical conclusions may be drawn from
'natural' premisses. Its weakness here was most clearly exposed, not by the more direct successors of Hobbes, but by
the new 'sentimental' school in which the leading figures
were Hutcheson and Hume. The arguments of these men were
directed against Clarke more than anyone else. For Butler they
had a certain respect; he shared with them an indebtedness
to Shaftesbury, and much of their point of view. Cudworth
they hardly mentioned; and it is not clear that Hutcheson
really disagreed (though it is clear that Hume did) with his
view that moral goodness and badness are real qualities in
actions; what he insisted upon was that their perception was
the work of an internal 'sense' rather than anything to which
he would consent to give the name of 'reason'; and that our
knowledge of their presence can never be wholly the result
of inference. When we speak of the 'reason for an action',
Hutcheson said, we either mean an 'exciting reason' or reason
why it is done, or a 'justifying reason' or reason why it is
approved, and 'all *exciting Reasons* pre-suppose *Instincts* and

Affections; and the *justifying* pre-suppose a *Moral Sense*.[1]
Reason may show us what actions will attain what ends; but
we pursue no ultimate ends without desiring them, and
approve none without immediately 'sensing' their goodness.

There is little or nothing in Hume's moral philosophy that
cannot be traced to Hutcheson, but in Hume it is all more
clear and pointed. And what is clearer from Hume's presentation of the 'sentimentalist' case is that there are certain
affinities between this position and certain elements in that
of Hobbes, though in other ways they are poles apart. Hume
rejected Hobbes's reduction of all men's motives to self-
interest (in this Shaftesbury, Butler, Hutcheson, and Hume
were all at one); but he shared Hobbes's tendency to reduce
the ethical question as to why all men ought to act in certain
ways to the psychological question as to why some men do
act in certain ways. Hume's moral precepts, like Hobbes's,
are 'theorems' or recipes, though recipes for the satisfaction
not only of our desire for security but also of our sympathy
or 'sentiment of humanity'. He was prepared to speak of
certain situations as 'calling for' certain actions, and of the
mind as perceiving that they do; but only in the sense that the
mind may perceive that in those situations certain actions
will best serve the ends set before us by our desires. 'We
speak not strictly and philosophically, when we talk of the
combat of passion and reason. Reason is, and ought only to
be, the slave of the passions, and can never pretend to any
other office than to serve and obey them.' And Hume freely
recognizes, as Hobbes sometimes seems reluctant to recognize, that this means that what actions a situation 'calls for'
will depend upon what our desires are, and will vary with
them. No one is interested in recipes for what he does not
want. 'It can never in the least concern us to know, that such
objects are causes, and such objects effects, if both the causes

[1] *Illustrations upon the Moral Sense*, i; Selby-Bigge, § 449.

and the effects be indifferent to us.'[1] And everything is 'indifferent' which does not awaken desire or aversion.

For Hume the distinction between virtue and vice is 'natural', in the sense that it is not merely created by agreement or decree. But the distinction does not mean, for him any more than for Hobbes, one between two contrasted qualities in the actions themselves; the contrast lies only in the emotions with which they are viewed.

'Take any action allowed to be vicious; wilful murder, for instance. Examine it in all lights, and see if you can find that matter of fact, or real existence, which you call *vice*. . . . The vice entirely escapes you, so long as you consider the object. You can never find it, till you turn your reflection into your own breast. . . . It lies in yourself, not in the object. So that when you pronounce any action or character to be vicious, you mean nothing, but that from the constitution of your nature you have a feeling or sentiment of blame from the contemplation of it.'

This follows inevitably from Hume's view that nothing but desire and aversion can move us to action, combined with the common view (which he accepts) that the rightness of an act is a motive for performing it, and its wrongness a motive for the contrary. Since 'reason is wholly inactive', it 'can never be the source of so active a principle as conscience'.[2] Hume thus draws together into a single broad argument for the subservience of reason to emotion Hutcheson's arguments for the dependence of 'exciting reasons' for action upon 'impulses and affections', and for the dependence of 'justifying reasons' upon a 'moral sense'. In Hume, more unambiguously than in Hutcheson, 'justification' is at bottom no more than a particular variety of 'excitement'.

From this standpoint, Hume exposes the complete inconsequence of the type of argument by which rationalism had come to be defended.

'In every system of morality which I have hitherto met with,

[1] *Treatise of Human Nature*, II. iii. 3.   [2] Ibid. III. i. 1.

I have always remarked, that the author proceeds for some time in the ordinary way of reasoning, and establishes the being of a God, or makes observations concerning human affairs; when, of a sudden, I am surprised to find, that, instead of the usual copulations of propositions, "is", and "is not", I meet with no proposition that is not connected with an "ought", or an "ought not". This change is imperceptible, but is, however, of the last consequence. For as this "ought" or "ought not" expresses some new relation or affirmation, it is necessary that it should be observed and explained: and, at the same time, that a reason should be given for what seems altogether inconceivable; how this new relation can be a deduction from others which are entirely different from it. But as authors do not commonly use this precaution, I shall presume to recommend it to the readers; and am persuaded, that this small attention would subvert all the vulgar systems of morality, and let us see that the distinction of vice and virtue is not founded merely on the relations of objects, nor is perceived by reason.'[1]

In this 'puckish passage', as Dr. Raphael calls it,[2] we have Cudworth's most cogent argument against Hobbes, turned against Cudworth's successors by one who may be regarded, from the points of view earlier indicated, as Hobbes's most logical disciple. But of course Hume's argument does not prove all that he claims for it—it exposes a weakness in some presentations of ethical rationalism, but does not overthrow ethical rationalism itself. So Hume too is inconsequent; and one of the first replies he met with, that of Thomas Reid, is at least as adequate as any that have been given since. Reid simply refuses to meet Hume's demand that the words 'ought' and 'ought not' be 'explained' ('To a man that understands English, there are surely no words that require explanation less'), or to show how ethical propositions may be deduced from non-ethical ones.

'The first principles of morals are not deductions. They are self-evident; and their truth, like that of other axioms, is perceived

---

[1] Ibid.   [2] *The Moral Sense*, p. 65.

without reasoning or deduction. And moral truths, that are not self-evident, are deduced, not from relations quite different from them, but from the first principles of morals.'[1]

As for the argument that the perception of an obligation cannot be a sufficient motive to action unless this so-called perception is in fact a desire, this is bound up with the question of free will. In Reid the 'motives' which solicit the will include not only 'animal motives' or desires, but 'rational motives' or perceived obligations; and a rational agent may resist a desire merely because he recognizes an obligation to do so, though he may also satisfy a desire in the face of an obligation not to—he may do either of these as he chooses; it is not just a case of automatically acting from the strongest desire. The view of Hutcheson and Hume that nothing but a desire can move the will to action is simply Hobbes's determinism.[2] Reid's view on the main point amounts, of course, to a frank abandonment of the attempt to find a 'foundation' for morality that is not itself already moral—it is an abandonment, that is to say, of the attempt to find a 'foundation' for the *whole* of morality.

The whole movement of opinion which has been traced in this study may be handily summarized by the employment of certain logical technicalities. The earlier ethical rationalists seem to have had in the back of their minds the following syllogism:

> All things discoverable by reason are capable of proof;
> And all ethical precepts are discoverable by reason;
> Therefore, all ethical precepts are capable of proof.

Now if a syllogism is valid (and this one certainly is), we cannot accept both premisses without accepting the conclusion; so that if we wish to accept one premiss and deny the conclusion, we must deny the other premiss; and this fact may be expressed in another syllogism. (This is the basis of

[1] *Essays on the Active Powers*, v. vii.   [2] Ibid. iv. iv.

the logical process known as the 'indirect reduction' of one syllogism to another.) If, for example, we accept the major premiss of the above syllogism, but cannot accept the conclusion, then we must abandon the minor premiss; and this fact may be expressed in the syllogism

> All things discoverable by reason are capable of proof;
> But not all ethical precepts are capable of proof;
> Therefore, not all ethical precepts are discoverable by reason.

And this expresses the reasoning of Hutcheson and Hume. But we could still deny the conclusion of the first syllogism without denying its minor premiss; only, if we do this, we must abandon the major premiss—a fact which may be expressed in a third syllogism, namely, the following:

> Not all ethical precepts are capable of proof;
> But all ethical precepts are discoverable by reason;
> Therefore, not all things discoverable by reason are capable of proof.

And this expresses the reasoning of Reid. The first of our three syllogisms, it may be noted, is in Figure 1, the figure most commonly used in the application of a general rule to a particular case asserted to fall under it (the minor premiss asserting that 'ethical precepts' fall under the rule applying to 'things discoverable by reason'); the second is in Figure 2, the figure most commonly used to show that a given case is not one falling under a certain general rule; and the third is in Figure 3, the figure most commonly used to show that something commonly taken to be a completely general rule is not so in reality.[1]

[1] See Keynes, *Formal Logic* (4th ed.), pp. 336–7.

IV

THE AUTONOMY OF ETHICS:
(3) SIDGWICK AND HIS CONTEMPORARIES

THE clarifications achieved through the ethical discussions of the eighteenth century were largely forgotten during the nineteenth, except by one or two, such as Archbishop Whately, who carried no great weight in the field of Moral Philosophy. But towards the end of the century we find the older and clearer language being spoken again by a moralist who commanded the attention of his fellows, namely, Henry Sidgwick; and in our own time the perception that information about our obligations cannot be logically derived from premises in which our obligations are not mentioned has become a commonplace, though perhaps only in philosophical circles. In this section and the next I shall bring the history of this perception up to date, the main matters requiring to be discussed on the way being (a) the relation to our present subject of Kant's distinction between categorical and hypothetical imperatives, and (b) a regrettable lapse of Mr. E. F. Carritt's from the 'party line' of consistent non-naturalism.

In Sidgwick there is far more than a revival of old positions; he develops them with a new subtlety, no doubt acquired in the process of threading his way through denser obscurities (in the work of his contemporaries) than any eighteenth-century writer had to cope with; but the positions which he thus develops are the old ones, and quite consciously so.

On the question now under consideration, Sidgwick's position is a critical rationalism, like that of Reid. He holds that Ethics, and also Politics (as distinct from Sociology), are 'distinguished from all positive sciences by having as their special and primary object to determine what ought to be, and not to ascertain what merely is, has been, or will be'. He admits that

'on any theory, our view of what ought to be must be largely derived, in details, from our apprehension of what is; the means of realising our ideal can only be thoroughly learnt by a careful study of actual phenomena; and to any individual asking himself "What ought I to do or aim at?" it is important to examine the answers which his fellow-men have actually given to similar questions. Still, it is clear that an attempt to ascertain the general laws or uniformities by which the varieties of human conduct, and of men's sentiments and judgments respecting conduct, may be explained, is essentially different from an attempt to determine which among these varieties of conduct is right and which of these divergent judgments valid. It is . . . the systematic consideration of these latter questions which constitutes, in my view, the special and distinct aim of Ethics and Politics.'[1]

Dealing with the notion of 'Conformity to Nature', he admits, again, that 'in a certain sense every rational man must . . . "conform to nature"; that is, in aiming at any ends, he must adapt his efforts to the particular conditions of his existence, physical and psychical'. But of the supposition that 'by contemplating the actual play of human impulses, or the physical constitution of man, or his social relations, we may find principles for determining positively and completely the kind of life he was designed to live', he says that 'every attempt thus to derive "what ought to be" from "what is" palpably fails, the moment it is freed from fundamental confusions of thought'.[2]

In expounding his point of view Sidgwick sometimes makes use of Kant's distinction between 'hypothetical' or conditional imperatives, which instruct us how best to achieve some end which we desire ('If you want X, you ought to do Y'), and 'categorical' or unconditional imperatives, which set before our reason what we ought to do, whether we desire

---

[1] *Methods of Ethics*, I. i. I.   [2] Ibid. vi. 2.

the state of affairs which such action will bring about or not. But Sidgwick makes some important modifications to Kant's doctrine. In Kant, an act which is 'categorically imperative' is so regardless of its consequences. But Sidgwick notes that a man might deny that he has any 'moral obligation to actions without reference to consequences', and yet might 'recognise some universal end or ends—whether it be the general happiness, or well-being otherwise understood—as that at which it is ultimately reasonable to aim, subordinating to its attainment the gratification of any personal desires that may conflict with this aim'. For such a person,

'the unconditional imperative plainly comes in as regards the end, which is—explicitly or implicitly—recognised as the end at which all men "ought" to aim; and it can hardly be denied that the recognition of an end as ultimately reasonable involves the recognition of an obligation to do such acts as most conduce to the end. The obligation is not indeed "unconditional", but it does not depend on the existence of any non-rational desires or aversions.'

Even those who recognize no duties but ones to promote some end (Sidgwick himself was one such) may distinguish between such a duty and a desire for the end. This distinction remains even when it is held that the only end which any man ought to pursue is his own greatest good or happiness; for this might be held by one who agreed with Butler[1] that 'men daily, hourly sacrifice the greatest known interest, to fancy, inquisitiveness, love or hatred, any vagrant inclination', and that 'the thing to be lamented is, not that men have so great regard to their own good or interest in the present world, for they have not enough'. 'Thus', Sidgwick says, 'the notion "ought"—as expressing the relation of rational judgment to non-rational impulses—will find a place in the practical rules of any egoistic system, no less than in the rules of ordinary morality, understood as prescribing duty without

[1] *Sermons on Human Nature*, Preface, 40.

reference to the agent's interest.' But he goes farther. Even imperatives which do 'depend on the existence of non-rational desires and aversions' presuppose a 'categorical' imperative of a sort.

'When (e.g.) a physician says, "If you wish to be healthy you ought to rise early", this is not the same thing as saying "early rising is an indispensable condition of the attainment of health." This latter proposition expresses the relation of physiological facts on which the former is founded; but it is not merely this relation of facts that the word "ought" imparts: it also implies the unreasonableness of adopting an end, and refusing to adopt the means indispensable to its attainment.'[1]

That such 'unreasonableness' is not psychologically impossible is one of Sidgwick's characteristic doctrines; he develops it not only at this point in *The Methods of Ethics*, but also, more fully, in his *Practical Ethics*.[2] And if a man holds that we 'ought' not to be thus unreasonable—if he holds that when we desire X more than we are averse to doing Y, and doing Y is the only means of obtaining X, then we 'ought' to do Y— such an 'ought' cannot be derived from the mere fact that Y *is* the only means of obtaining X; it too is, if not a 'categorical' obligation, at all events an underived one (unless, of course, it is derived from yet another obligation).

Sidgwick's purpose here is not to criticize Kant but rather to show how difficult it is *not* to recognize a 'categorical imperative' of some sort. He admits that he knows no way to 'impart the notion of moral obligation to anyone who is entirely devoid of it'; but he makes it clear that one has to look very far to find such a person. He drives the notion from its very last hiding-place in those who really possess it but claim that they do not. But since in so doing he finds the notion to be involved in imperatives which Kant classified as hypothetical as much as in those which he called categorical,

---

[1] *Methods of Ethics*, I. iii. 4.   [2] *Essay* IX.

the inevitable effect of his procedure is to leave one wondering whether Kant's comparison of the distinction between obligations and desires with that between categorical and hypothetical propositions is really a very appropriate one. Kant's categorical imperatives are universal rules—'All rational beings ought (or ought not) to do so and so'—and it is now recognized by most logicians that all ordinary universal propositions are hypothetical in meaning even when they are not so in form. 'All S is P', or 'Everything that is S is P', is only a way of saying '*If* anything is S it is P'. It is certainly not difficult to formulate the kinds of imperative which Kant regarded as categorical, in this hypothetical way. 'You ought to keep your promises', for example, plainly means the same as 'If you have promised to do anything, you ought to do it'.[1] The categorical form suggested to Kant that he had obtained rules which were binding regardless of circumstances as well as of consequences; but even the one just given, when fully set out, is seen to be conditional on the promise having been made, and if this is relevant to the obligation, other circumstances may be so too. 'Circumstances' always enter, to a greater or less degree, into the very definition of the class of acts asserted to be obligatory. (British ethical rationalists have nearly always recognized this—they speak of right action as that which 'the state of the case requires', and so on—and this seems to me one of their main points of superiority to Kant.) 'You ought not to tell lies', similarly, seems to mean something like 'If you believe that any utterance will deceive any one, you ought not to give voice to it'. And if these imperatives are nevertheless to count as 'categorical', then there can be no objection in principle to allowing the same status to Sidgwick's one, 'If anything will promote the

[1] This hypothetical element in the duty of promise-keeping is emphasized by Cudworth in the passage quoted on p. 19; though Cudworth did not perceive any more than Kant did that all moral rules whatever might be expressed as hypothetical propositions.

general happiness, you ought to do it'; or even to 'If you desire X more than you are averse to doing Y, and doing Y is the only way to obtain X, you ought to do Y'.

The only obligations that are in all logical strictness 'categorical' are the actual ones that lie on particular persons at particular moments, e.g. 'It is now incumbent on me to pay this man some money.' These may be derived from 'general' obligations or moral rules, i.e. from the kind of imperatives which we have now seen to be all hypothetical, by adding a categorical premiss about our actual situation, thus,

> If any debt falls due at any time, it ought to be paid at
> that time,
> And this debt falls due now;
> Therefore, this debt ought to be paid now.

If we had not the first of these premisses, we could not draw an ethical conclusion (for the second premiss says nothing about our obligations); and if we had not the second, we could not draw a categorical one (for the first premiss is only conditional). I am not suggesting that it is by making inferences of this kind that we normally come to learn what our categorical obligations are. On the contrary, it seems likely that we come to know what responses situations of a given kind demand, i.e. we come to apprehend moral rules, only through being in a particular situation of the sort in question, and perceiving then and there the particular obligation which its character imposes upon us. And even then, we may not be able to discuss with any precision how the various elements in the situation determine the obligation to which it gives rise; so that we may be able to formulate no rule more helpful than the one that any situation of exactly the same character would give rise to the same obligation; and for practical guidance we may have to depend on intuition or guess-work in each case as it arises.[1] But it remains true that a mistake

[1] See Carritt's *Theory of Morals*, pp. 114–17.

about either (*a*) the kind of situation we are in, or (*b*) the obligation to which that kind of situation gives rise, can and often does lead, by a valid process of inference, to a mistaken view of our present categorical obligation; and also that our true present obligation could be automatically inferred from (*a*) and (*b*) if complete knowledge of these were ever attainable.

Actual cases of obligations derived from the rule that we ought to do what is indispensable to the satisfaction of our strongest desires are just as 'categorical' as any others. Consider, for example, the inference,

> If those who desire health more than they are averse to rising early can only achieve health by rising early, they ought to rise early.
> Mr. A desires health more than he is averse to rising early, and can only achieve health by rising early.
> Therefore, Mr. A ought to rise early.

The inference is of exactly the same sort as the one given in the preceding paragraph, and its conclusion is just as 'categorical'. (If the truth of the conclusion is doubtful, that is because the truth of the first premiss—the 'hypothetical imperative'—is doubtful; and the truth of the conclusion of the inference in the preceding paragraph is doubtful for the same reason. There may be desires which we ought not to satisfy even when they are stronger than our aversion to the means of satisfying them; there may also be debts which we ought not to pay when they fall due.) The really important distinction is not that between 'If you want X, you ought to do Y' and, say, 'If you have promised to do Y, you ought to do Y', but that between both of these and 'If you do not do Y, you will not get what you want'. The latter is a purely causal assertion in which not even a conditional obligation to do Y is mentioned, whereas both the former are about obligations. And if this is the distinction which Kant really meant by his one between hypothetical and categorical imperatives, one can only say that that is a very loose way of describing it. It was one of Sidgwick's outstanding merits that, although he used the Kantian terminology, it did not mislead him as to where the really important line was to be drawn.

Sidgwick's sharp distinction between the 'normative' study of Ethics and all 'positive' sciences was given a special application by his younger associate at Cambridge, Dr. J. N. Keynes, in the second chapter of the latter's work on *The Scope and Method of Political Economy*.[1] Dr. Keynes insists here on 'the possibility of studying economic laws or uniformities without passing ethical judgments or formulating economic precepts'. Such laws or uniformities, in other words, do not in themselves commit their discoverers to any judgement as to what is good or ought to be done; that is, no such judgements are deducible from them. This is definitely not to 'claim for economic action a sphere altogether independent of moral laws'. It is quite fallacious to imagine that the placing of economic activities beyond the scope of moral criticism is in any way a logical consequence of 'the attempt to construct a purely positive science of economics'. On the contrary, 'it is rather the failure to recognise the fundamentally distinct character of enquiries into what is, and enquiries into what ought to be, that is really responsible for attempts to solve practical economic questions without reference to their ethical aspects'. It is just because 'pure' economics studies factual uniformities alone, and because no directions for practice can be inferred from such uniformities alone, that such directions cannot be obtained without a reference to ethics as well as economics.

The positive study can, of course, aid us in arriving at detailed practical decisions.

'It is clear, for example, that we cannot determine how nearly the results of free competition approximate to our economic ideal' —i.e. to the form of economic life which our ethical views lead us

---

[1] Especially § 2, from which the passages quoted here are taken.

to regard as desirable—'until we know what those results are. Nor can we say how far it is desirable that the effects which would be brought about by unimpeded competition should be modified by governmental interference or voluntary combination, until we have also ascertained what kind of modification would ensue, and what would be the collateral effects of such interfering agencies.'

But the ideal itself cannot arise from such knowledge of how best to attain it. 'Economic precepts', therefore, must be carefully distinguished from 'the theorems of the positive science upon which they are based'—they must be thus distinguished, because they can never be more than partly based on these 'theorems'; they are not just further 'theorems' deduced from them. The theorems say, 'if you have free competition', or whatever it may be, 'the results will be so and so'. They are, in fact, the economic counterpart of the 'theorems' of Hobbes, which say, 'If you do so and so, you will have peace, and preserve your lives.' And as in the case of the theorems of Hobbes, the practical use we make of them will depend on the kind of persons we are, or on what we take our obligations to be.

Dr. Keynes also admits that even 'from the purely positive standpoint, the operation of moral forces may need to be taken into account'. It may be necessary to 'enquire in detail in what ways economic phenomena are or may be affected by the pressure of public opinion, or by motives of justice, and kindliness, and concern for the general well-being'. But 'to recognise the influence, actual or potential, exerted by the economic ideals that men may frame for themselves is not the same thing as to discuss the objective validity of those ideals'.

We find the same general emphasis in the famous Romanes Lecture of T. H. Huxley on *Evolution and Ethics*, recently reprinted and edited by his grandson. If pure economics is in itself incompetent to tell us what we ought to do, so is evolutionary biology. Biologically, 'the thief and the murderer follow nature just as much as the philanthropist.

Cosmic evolution may teach us how the good and the evil tendencies in man have come about; but, in itself, it is incompetent to furnish us with any better reason why what we call good is preferable to what we call evil than we had before.'[1] The Stoics also, he notices, claimed to base their ethics on a theory of cosmic evolution. But 'so far as I can see, the ethical system of the Stoics, which is essentially intuitive, and reveres the categorical imperative as strongly as that of any later moralists, might have been just what it was if they had held any other theory'.[2]

Huxley acquired a certain celebrity or notoriety, not only as a critic of attempts to turn Ethics into 'applied Natural History', but also as an opponent of Christianity; and it is common for theologians to-day to refer to him as occupying a position which is now impossible, in which the Christian moral code is retained despite the loss of the Christian faith. It is now plain, we are told, that when Christian theology goes, Christian ethics must go too; if we wish to retain the latter, we must return to the former. But while it may very well be true that ethical standards lose their hold on men when religious faith and hope disappear, it seems to me that Huxley was plainly right in insisting that there is no *logical* dependence of any system of moral precepts upon either religion or science, i.e. that the former cannot be deduced from the latter. This would, I think, have been the verdict of an older theology too; though a certain amount of ethics is usually included in theological systems, so that the question for the believer is not so much whether ethics may be 'based' on theology, as whether the ethical part of theology—say, the doctrine of God's moral authority over men—may be 'based' on the non-ethical part of it—say, the doctrine of His power. We have already seen how Cudworth handled this question; and we shall encounter it again.

---

[1] *Evolution and Ethics 1893–1943*, by T. H. Huxley and Julian Huxley, p. 80. [2] Ibid. p. 78.

V

PROMISING AS SPECIAL CREATION

In the earlier part of the present century the type of view
which we have been considering found provocative expression in the late Professor Prichard's article entitled, 'Does
Moral Philosophy Rest on a Mistake?'[1] In Prichard's view
it was a 'mistake' to attempt to 'rest' morality on anything at
all. His position was Reid's rather than Hume's, but, like
Reid, he was close to Hume on the logic of the matter. Dr.
Raphael has pointed out[2] that all that is really cogent in
Hume's remarks about 'ought' and 'ought not' is contained
in Prichard's observation that 'an "ought", if it is to be
derived at all, can only be derived from another "ought" '.
Prichard was also at one with Hume in his view of the
positive but essentially subsidiary part which inference may
play in the settlement of moral questions.

'The plausibility of the view that obligations are not self-evident
but need proof lies in the fact that an act which is referred to as
an obligation may be incompletely stated. If, e.g., we refer to the
act of repaying X by a present merely as giving X a present, it
appears, and indeed is, necessary to give a reason. In other
words, whenever a moral act is regarded in this incomplete way
the question, "*Why* should I do it?" is perfectly legitimate. This
fact suggests, but suggests wrongly, that even if the nature of the
act is completely stated, it is still necessary to give a reason, or, in
other words, to supply a proof.'[3]

Hume also says that

'all the circumstances of the case are supposed to be laid before
us, ere we can fix any sentence of blame or approbation. If any
material circumstance be yet unknown or doubtful, we must first
employ our inquiry or intellectual faculties to assure us of it;

[1] *Mind*, 1912.   [2] *The Moral Sense*, p. 95n.
[3] *Mind*, 1912, p. 28.

and must suspend for a time all moral decision or sentiment. While we are ignorant, whether a man were aggressor or not, how can we determine whether the person who killed him, be criminal or innocent? But after every circumstance, every relation is known, the understanding has no further room to operate, nor any object on which it could employ itself. The approbation or blame which then ensues, cannot be the work of the judgment, but of the heart; and is not a speculative proposition or affirmation, but an active feeling or sentiment.'[1]

Prichard would no doubt have agreed with Reid's blunt reply to the last sentence or two, that 'the man who deliberates, after all the objects and relations mentioned by Mr. Hume are known to him, has a point to determine; and that is, whether the action under his deliberation ought to be done or ought not';[2] but he would still have agreed, as Reid himself would have agreed, with Hume's insistence that this final question is not determined by a process of inference from the answers given to the rest.

There is, however, in the latest work of one writer of Prichard's school, Mr. E. F. Carritt, what seems to be a regression to the less critical rationalism of the period immediately prior to that of Hume. It is not quite that, as there is a similar lapse, at the same point, in Reid. In discussing the duty of keeping promises and contracts Reid argues that since 'the will to become bound, and to confer a right upon the other party, is . . . the very essence of a contract', it is self-contradictory to give our word and at the same time deny that we are obliged to keep it; for that 'would be the same as if one should say, I promise to do such a thing, but I do not promise'.[3] If this is so, the obligation to keep a promise can be demonstrated from the mere fact that it has been made. Mr. Carritt similarly argues that 'a man could not without self-contradiction make a promise while explaining that he

---

[1] *Enquiry concerning the Principles of Morals*, Appendix I.
[2] *Essays on the Active Powers*, v. vii.   [3] Ibid. v. vi.

was under no obligation to keep it';[1] for 'I promise' *means* 'I hereby place myself under an obligation'.[2]

There is a suspicious resemblance between Mr. Carritt's description of a promise and the absurd description of a lawful command which Cudworth puts into the mouth of an imaginary follower of Hobbes. 'I hereby place myself under an obligation to do X' is only slightly different in form from 'I hereby place *you* under an obligation to do X'. A promise is a kind of command addressed to one's own future self. 'The will of another', says Cudworth, 'doth no more oblige in commands than our own will in promises and covenants.'[3] But Mr. Carritt thinks that our own will does lay obligations upon us in promises and covenants, meaning by this something more radical than that it causes some specific act to 'fall under' the already existing general obligation to keep promises. And unlike the ethical rationalists of the early eighteenth century, he is aware that he is reproducing at this point one of the characteristic positions of Hobbes. For he finds a foreshadowing of his own view in the suggestion of Hobbes that

'*Injury*, or *Injustice*, in the controversies of the world, is somewhat like to that, which in the disputations of the Scholars is called an Absurdity. For as it is there called an Absurdity to contradict what one maintained in the Beginning; so in the world, it is called Injustice and Injury, voluntarily to undo that, which from the beginning he hath voluntarily done.'[4]

Now although I think Mr. Carritt, when he writes about promising, shares Hobbes's illusion that an obligation may be inferred from something that is not an obligation (in this case, from an *assertion that we have* an obligation), I am not sure that what Mr. Carritt says of promising is quite the same as what Hobbes says in the passage quoted. What Hobbes

---

[1] *Ethical and Political Thinking*, p. 37.   [2] Ibid., p. 102.
[3] *Treatise concerning Eternal and Immutable Morality*, I. ii. 4.
[4] *Leviathan*, ch. 14.

says is that there is a certain analogy between the acts of making promises and breaking them, and those of making assertions and denying them; but what Mr. Carritt says is that to make a promise and, not to break it, but to deny that it is binding, is not merely analogous to, but is a particular case of, making an assertion and denying it. A promise asserts that we have an obligation, and to deny that we are obliged to keep the promise is, in Mr. Carritt's view, to deny that we have that very obligation which the promise asserts that we have. But even if Mr. Carritt were right about this, might not the denial that we have the obligation be true, and the assertion that we have the obligation—i.e. the promise itself—be false? It is at this point that the real peculiarity of Mr. Carritt's view appears; for he says that a promise is the kind of proposition that cannot be false.

The statement 'I hereby place myself under an obligation', Mr. Carritt tells us, is like the statement 'I am making a statement'; and indeed it is; but what is not so certain, in either case, is that the statement cannot be false, or even that it is really a statement at all. 'I am making a statement' means, I take it, that there is some specific statement that I am making when I utter the words; and although I do not say what it is, presumably I know; for if I do not, certainly no one else does; and if no one knows what the statement is, perhaps there isn't any, and then 'I am making a statement' would be false. But Mr. Carritt says it cannot be false; and it is plain enough that the answer he intends us to give to the question '*What* statement am I making?' is 'I am making the statement that I am making a statement'. But *what* statement am I making the statement that I am making? The only answer which would make the expression infallibly true would appear to be that I am making the statement that I am making the statement that I am making a statement. There is plainly no end to all this—this 'statement', if it is a statement at all, is a bottomless abyss. And similarly, when I say that I 'hereby' place myself under an obligation, I must mean that there is some specific act by which I place myself under this obligation. What is it? Mr. Carritt's meaning plainly is that I place myself under this obligation by the act of 'promising'—i.e. by 'hereby placing myself under an obligation.' But once again—*whereby*? I think the vicious infinite regress in which Mr. Carritt is involved escapes his notice because he imagines that he is entitled to answer the first 'Whereby?' by saying, 'By placing myself under this obligation.' For a little farther on in the paragraph which opens with his definition he speaks of 'our description of a promise as "putting oneself under an obligation"'. But this is changing the definition by omitting the 'hereby'; and the 'hereby' is important, for 'putting oneself under an obligation' would plainly not be accepted by Mr. Carritt or anyone else as a complete description of 'promising'—there are many other ways of putting oneself under an obligation besides promising, in any ordinary sense of 'promising'.

The sentence by which Mr. Carritt translates 'I promise' suffers from a defect which Russell and Whitehead call ambiguity as to its 'logical type'.[1] It is not clear whether it is a statement about an object, or a statement about a statement; or perhaps more accurately, it is not clear whether it is a statement about an object, or is itself the object which the statement is about. I have, accordingly, dealt with it by what is substantially Russell and Whitehead's method; and this would seem to be one of the points at which, for the efficient conduct of ethical controversy, 'Aristotle is not enough'. I suspect, nevertheless, that there are neglected portions of older logical systems in which the 'theory of types' is already adumbrated. (Some of William of Ockham's distinctions perhaps come close to it.) At all events, more than a century and a half before the *Principia Mathematica* appeared, David Hume made the same criticism as I have

[1] *Principia Mathematica*, Introduction, ch. ii.

made of the same theory of promising as Mr. Carritt's.
The latter, indeed, quotes Hume, along with Hobbes, in his
own support. Hume does say that a promise is 'a certain
form of word . . . by which we bind ourselves to the performance of an action'. But he does not mean by this what Mr.
Carritt means by it; what he does mean we shall see shortly.
He explicitly disowns, as a 'manifest absurdity', the theory
that the obligation to keep promises 'arises from our mere
will and pleasure'. He thinks this untenable from either
a sentimentalist or a rationalist point of view. On his own
view, 'all morality depends upon our sentiments. . . . A change
of the obligation supposes a change of the sentiment; and
a creation of a new obligation supposes some new sentiment
to arise. But it is certain we can naturally no more change
our own sentiments than the motions of the heavens.' But
he observes in a footnote that 'were morality discoverable
by reason, and not by sentiment, it would be still more
evident that promises could make no alteration upon it'. For,
by rationalists such as Clarke,

'morality is supposed to consist in relations. Every new imposi-
tion of morality, therefore, must arise from some new relation of
objects. . . . To will a new obligation is to will a new relation of
objects; and therefore, if this new relation of objects were formed
by the volition itself, we should, in effect, will the volition, which
is plainly absurd and impossible. The will has here no object to
which it could tend, but must return upon itself *in infinitum*.
The new obligation depends upon new relations. The new relations depend upon a new volition. The new volition has for
object a new obligation, and consequently new relations, and
consequently a new volition; which volition, again, has in view
a new obligation, relation, and volition, without any termination.'[1]

We may paraphrase Hume's argument, or rather Hume's
representation of the rationalist argument, as follows: In
a situation which in itself gives rise to no obligation to do X,

[1] *Treatise*, III. ii. 5.

we resolve to alter the situation so that it does give rise to such an obligation. But in what respect do we resolve to alter the situation? We resolve to alter it by inserting into it a resolve to alter the situation so that it gives rise to an obligation to do X. By inserting into it a resolve to alter the situation in what respect? By inserting into it a resolve to alter, &c., &c.

The difficulty about what people generally mean by promising is that it is something more than merely announcing what our intentions are, since the obligation to keep a promise is in some way more stringent than the obligation to announce our intentions truly. There is as it were an added solemnity about such an announcement when it takes the form of a promise. Hence we come to imagine that a promise to do X conveys some additional information that is not conveyed by the mere assertion that we intend or have resolved to do X; and so, as Hume puts it, 'we *feign* a new act of the mind, which we call the *willing* an obligation', i.e. the creation of an obligation by the mere resolve to do so, though in fact, 'there is no such act of the mind', and cannot be. Hume's own view, which seems to me substantially correct, is that while a promise to do X is *something more than a statement* of our intention to do X, it is not a *statement of something more* than our intention to do X. To give one's word is not merely to make a statement but to perform a ritual act, and it is this which brings us under a special obligation. That is what Hume means by calling a promise 'a *certain form of word* . . . by which we bind ourselves to the performance of any action'. He compares it with the priest's words of consecration in the Roman Catholic Mass, though he gives it a more rational basis—the formula by which a man gives his word derives its obliging force from the particularly confident expectation which its common use creates. 'By making use of this *form of words*', a man 'subjects himself to the penalty of never being trusted again in case of failure'. Perhaps the non-informative element in promising might be most accurately expressed by some non-indicative form of speech, such as 'Let me never be trusted again if I do not do X'. (Such non-indicative modes of speech will be again encountered in my seventh study.)

It is necessary to distinguish this view of Hume's as to what we mean by promises, from his view as to what we mean by the obligation to keep them. Hume reduces obligations in general to desires and tendencies; and the obligation to keep promises, to a tendency in men to keep them, and to make others do so, arising from the known convenience of being able to trust and be trusted by our fellows, at least on the special occasions marked by this 'form of words'. But even a man who rejects this account of obligation, and who regards the obligation to keep promises as a 'first principle of morals' in Reid's sense, might still agree that what distinguishes a promise from a mere statement of an intention is something non-informative. It is no doubt their dislike of Hume's reduction of the duty of promise-keeping to expediency which has blinded rationalistic moralists to the merits of his positive account of what promising is, as well as to the cogency of his criticism of alternative accounts, of the type now revived by Mr. Carritt.

VI

PROPRIETY AND TRUTH:
(1) PRELIMINARY HISTORY

IN this study and the next two I propose to consider more
fully a view of which some hints have already appeared,
namely, the view that there is some special analogy or even
identity between wrongness in action and falsehood or self-
contradiction in theory. This analogy is made by Hobbes in
the passage quoted by Mr. Carritt as an anticipation of his
own account of the obligation to keep promises; but in
Hobbes it appears only as a rather desperate device of a man
who half-sees the impossibility of any other way of founding
obligations upon what are not obligations—it does not
represent his usual ways of thinking. In Clarke, the thought
that 'Iniquity is the very same in action, as falsity or contradiction in theory'[1] is a fairly frequently repeated one.
'Wilfully to act contrary to known justice and equity', he says
again, is 'to will things to be what they are not and cannot
be.'[2] This seems to mean that (a) a man who does what is
wrong must wish it were right, and (b) for what is wrong to
be right, a thing would have to be what it is not and cannot
be. The latter of these assertions is ambiguous in a way that
has already been fully discussed; and Clarke's grounds for
the former are obscure.

What was not much more than a loose and extravagant
way of speaking in Hobbes and Clarke was turned by one of
the latter's disciples, William Wollaston, into a quite precise
moral theory. Wollaston took over from Clarke the view that
the rightness of an action consists in its 'propriety', i.e. its
fitness or suitableness to the situation in which it is performed; or, as Butler put it, in its being 'what the state of the

[1] *Discourse upon Natural Religion*, i. 4; Selby-Bigge, 500.
[2] Ibid. 3; Selby-Bigge, 490.

case requires'. But Wollaston was not content to leave it at that; he had to give the fundamental relation of 'moral appropriateness' or 'being called-for' a definition, and in order to do so he made a certain important assertion or assumption. He pointed out that propositions may be framed, i.e. that information may be conveyed, by gestures as well as by speech and writing; and went on from that to assert that everything we do is in fact a gesture. All our actions are propositions—all our actions assert something. And they all assert something, in particular, about the situations in which they are performed. Wollaston's definition of right and wrong is simply this: If what an action says about the situation in which it is performed is true, then that act is suitable to the situation, 'in accordance with the nature of things', or right; if what it says is false, it is unsuitable or wrong. To fire on a body of men, for example, is in effect to declare that they are our enemies; if they are not, we have 'acted a lie', and so have acted wrongly.[1]

Some people are so constituted that the fallacy in this system is evident to them at a glance; but Wollaston ought not to be underestimated. Butler described him as an 'author of great and deserved reputation',[2] and made no criticism of his positive theory, though he attempted to answer his criticism of those who 'place all in following nature'. Wollaston says of these that, if what they mean by the phrase is just his own theory—if they mean by following nature, 'treating things as being what they in nature are, or according to truth'—he has, of course, no objections.[3]

'But this does not seem to be their meaning. And if it is only that a man must follow his own nature, since his nature is not purely rational, but there is a part of him, which he has in common with brutes, they appoint him a guide which I fear will

[1] *The Religion of Nature Delineated*, I. iii; Selby-Bigge, 1026.
[2] *Sermons*, Preface, 13.
[3] *The Religion of Nature Delineated*, I. ix; Selby-Bigge, 1046.

mislead him, this being commonly more likely to prevail, than the rational part. At best this talk is loose.'

Butler's description of our moving impulses as being 'naturally' arranged in a hierarchy was elaborated as an answer to this; but, for reasons indicated in an earlier study, I doubt whether the answer will bear examination. And if Wollaston's alternative to 'following nature' will not bear examination either, it has never, in one form or another, wanted adherents. Not only the earlier extravagances of Cudworth and Clarke, but many subsequent ethical theories, have been adumbrations of his central idea. It is present, for example, in Kant's well-known view that a right action must be one which we can 'without self-contradiction' imagine as performed by every rational being; and there are others who have come still closer to him, with whom I shall be dealing in detail. And Wollaston's presentation of this idea has at least the merit of clarity and simplicity.

For this last, one might have thought his opponents would have been grateful; but their first reactions to him were a series of angry and not very coherent or relevant splutterings. Thus we find Hutcheson labouring the point that we can make up as many true propositions about wrong actions as we can about right ones.

'Whatever *Attribute* can be ascribed to a *generous kind Action*, the *contrary Attribute* may be ascribed to a *selfish cruel Action*. Both propositions are equally *true*, and the two contrary Actions, the Objects of the two *Truths*, are equally *conformable* to their several Truths, with that sort of *Conformity* which is between a Truth and its Object.'[1]

This, of course, does not touch Wollaston, who does not deny that true propositions may be framed about wrong actions; in fact, he considers his own work to be full of them. What he says is not that some proposition about a wrong

[1] *Illustrations upon the Moral Sense*, i; Selby-Bigge, 448.

action, but that the proposition which a wrong action is, is false.

The clearest exposure of the real defect in Wollaston's system is to be found, as might be expected, in Hume. In all such arguments as Wollaston's, he points out, 'there is an evident reasoning in a circle. . . . A man that is ungrateful to his benefactor, in a manner affirms that he never received any favours from him. But in what manner? Is it because it is his duty to be grateful? But this supposes that there is some antecedent rule of duty and morals.'[1] To put the same argument in another way: The real difficulty about Wollaston's system is to decide in each case just what the action being considered asserts. And the method which Wollaston himself adopts, without being conscious that he is doing so, is perfectly obvious. If a man is not grateful to another, he asserts in effect that he has no duty to be grateful (this is like Clarke's assumption that when a man does what he knows is wrong, he wishes it were right); but (since we ought to be grateful to benefactors) this could only be true if the other had conferred no favours upon him; so that ingratitude in effect asserts that no favours have been conferred. He can then say that if favours have been conferred, what the action in effect asserts is false, and so the action is wrong; but he can only arrive at this conclusion because he has already assumed (in order to determine what the action asserts) that we ought to be grateful to benefactors.

Hume has a further argument against what he calls 'this whimsical system', namely, that 'it leaves us under the same difficulty to give a reason why truth is virtuous and falsehood vicious, as to account for the merit or turpitude of any other action. I shall allow, if you please, that all morality is derived from this supposed falsehood in action, provided you can give me any plausible reason why such a falsehood is immoral.' This, I think, amounts to charging Wollaston with

[1] *Treatise of Human Nature*, III. i. 1, first footnote.

the 'naturalistic fallacy'. Even if all wrong actions do assert
falsehoods, Hume argues, their asserting falsehoods is one
thing, and their wrongness is another; to ask whether lying is
wrong is still an intelligible question—if it were not, the
assertion that lying is always wrong would not be a significant
statement.

The more hard-headed ethical rationalists who came immediately after Hume did not attempt to revive Wollaston's
theory. One of them, indeed, Richard Price, simply makes
Hume's main criticisms of Wollaston his own.[1] Where the
theory next appeared was rather in the other camp—among
the followers of Hutcheson and Hume—and traces of it are
still to be found there. In order to observe accurately the
migration of this particular little flock of fallacies into its new
territory, we must first look more closely at that territory
itself.

The conclusion which Price drew from the fact that the
relation of moral appropriateness or rightness is demonstrably
other than that between a proposition and the fact which
renders it true, was that this relation is *sui generis*—that it is
a 'non-natural' one, which cannot be further defined.[2] This
was not, of course, the conclusion which Hume drew; which
was rather that there is no such relation—not, at least,
between an act and its circumstances considered in themselves. To call an act proper or fitting meant, for him, merely
that, when all its circumstances were known, it awakened in
the beholder a certain kind of agreeable feeling. But in this
'subjectivism' there is a certain ambiguity. What is not clear
is the degree of self-consciousness which is taken to be involved in moral judgement. When an object evokes a feeling
of approval in us, we may or may not be aware that it has
done so; or at all events, we may or may not direct our attention to the fact; and the phrase 'discerning the goodness of

---

[1] *Review of the Principal Questions in Morals*, Raphael's edition, p. 126;
Selby-Bigge, 693 and 694.   [2] See Note A, p. 108.

X' may be taken to mean the rather self-conscious 'discerning that we feel approval towards X', or it may be taken to mean simply 'feeling approval towards X'. On the former view, 'that X is good' means 'that I feel approval towards X', and 'good' itself means 'evoking approval in me'; on the latter view, the proposition 'that X is good', and the predicate 'good', when either is taken in isolation, have no meaning at all, though the complete phrase 'judging that X is good' has the meaning of 'feeling approval towards X'. The word 'good', on this second, more direct view, cannot be given a definition in the ordinary sense, i.e. it cannot be defined in isolation, though it may be given what Russell and Whitehead, in *Principia Mathematica*,[1] call a 'definition in use', i.e. the meaning of a phrase using the word may be identified with that of a quite different phrase not using it. It is because the second phrase is different *in toto* from the first that an ordinary definition, in these cases, cannot be given. If an assertion about one term is equated with *the same* assertion about another, then plainly we have equated the terms themselves, and can use one as a definition of the other. If we can say that 'eating Murphies' means 'eating potatoes', then we can say that 'Murphy' means 'potato'. But if—to take the standard *Principia Mathematica* example, the definition of 'class'—we can only say that 'being a member of the class of men' means 'possessing the quality of humanity', then we cannot identify the class of men with the quality of humanity or with anything else in the defining phrase. And the same difference, in regard to the definability of 'good', is involved in the two formulations of subjectivism. If 'I judge that X is good' means 'I judge that X is evoking approval in me', then 'good' can be defined as 'evoking approval in me'; but if the sentence means 'I feel approval towards X', then 'good', by itself, cannot be defined at all.

The distinction between these two versions or formulations

[1] Introduction, ch. iii.

of subjectivism is made very clearly by Thomas Reid. Reid argues in one passage that a disciple of Hume is bound to hold either that the proposition 'Such a man did well and worthily' means the same as 'This man's conduct gave me a very agreeable feeling', or that it means nothing at all. The former interpretation is unplausible, since the proposition 'Such a man did well and worthily', on the face of it, says nothing whatever about the feelings of the person who utters it; and if it were equivalent to a statement about his feelings, it would be impertinent to contradict it, since presumably the speaker has a better idea of what his own feelings are than anyone else has; but when we question a person's statement that 'Such a man did well and worthily', we do not usually think we are accusing the person of lying about his feelings. But if the 'judgement' expressed in this proposition is not one *about* the speaker's feelings, but is itself a feeling of the speaker, then the proposition can have no meaning at all, since what is merely felt cannot be expressed in a proposition.

'A feeling must be agreeable, or uneasy, or indifferent. It may be weak or strong. It is expressed in language either by a single word, or by such a contexture of words as may be the subject or predicate of a proposition, but such as cannot by themselves make a proposition. For it implies neither affirmation nor negation; and therefore cannot have the qualities of true or false, which distinguish propositions from all other forms of speech, and judgments from all other acts of the mind. *That I have such a feeling*, is indeed an affirmative proposition. . . . But the feeling is only one term of this proposition; and it can only make a proposition when joined with another term, by a verb affirming or denying.'[1]

To identify moral judgement with a feeling is therefore, in effect, to deny that it is a judgement at all; so Reid expresses his ultimate disagreement with Hume in his chapter-heading, 'That Moral Approbation implies a real Judgment.'

[1] *Essays on the Active Powers*, Essay V, ch. vii.

Of the two possible subjectivist accounts of moral judgement which Reid thus distinguishes, Hume sometimes adopts one and sometimes the other.[1] He even passes immediately from one to the other as if they were the same. He says, for instance, that 'to have the sense of virtue, is nothing but to *feel* a satisfaction of a particular kind arising from the contemplation of a character. The very *feeling* constitutes our praise or admiration'. But in the next sentence but one he says that 'in feeling that' a character 'pleases after such a particular manner we in effect feel that it is virtuous'.[2] Although he still uses the word 'feel' here, he has plainly moved from the strict psychological sense of the word to the popular one in which it is synonymous with 'immediately judge'—he now speaks, not of 'feeling a satisfaction', but of 'feeling that' something is the case; and he identifies the 'feeling' or judgement that the character is virtuous with the judgement that it gives satisfaction.[3] But however he may vacillate in his classification or definition of moral 'judgement', Hume is as eager as Reid to emphasize the difference in kind between a genuine judgement and a feeling, and the latter's incapability of being true or false. In his argument against the possibility of any conflict between 'passion' and reason, he says that whereas a judgement points beyond itself, claiming to be a perception of the real characters of objects, and this claim may be pronounced by our reason to be warranted or unwarranted, emotions make no such claims,

---

[1] See J. N. Findlay, *Mind*, 1944, p. 146. [2] *Treatise*, III. i. 2.
[3] Attention has been drawn to this passage in Hume's *Treatise* by Dr. Raphael, in *The Moral Sense*, p. 76, n. 2; but Dr. Raphael gives *both* parts of it as illustrating Hume's anticipation of a modern subjectivist's identification of moral judgement with a feeling. He fails to notice that there are two views in the passage, because he does not clearly distinguish between the contrast we are here making, and the contrast between the view that 'X is good' means 'The contemplation of X gives *me* satisfaction', and the view that it means 'The contemplation of X would give satisfaction to all or most men'. This last view is also sometimes attributed to Hume; we shall consider it later.

and there is therefore no point at which they are exposed to reason's criticism.

'A passion is an original existence, or, if you will, modification of existence, and contains not any representative quality, which renders it a copy of any other existence or modification. When I am angry, I am actually possessed with the passion, and in that emotion have no more reference to any other object, than when I am thirsty, or sick, or more than five feet high. It is impossible, therefore, that this passion can be opposed by, or be contradictory to truth and reason; since this contradiction consists in the disagreement of ideas, considered as copies, with those objects which they represent.'[1]

He extends the same principle to actions.

'Reason is the discovery of truth or falsehood. Truth or falsehood consists in an agreement or disagreement either to the *real* relations of ideas, or to *real* existence and matter of fact. . . . Now, it is evident our passions, volitions, and actions, are not susceptible of any such agreement or disagreement; being original facts and realities, complete in themselves, and implying no reference to other passions, volitions and actions. It is impossible, therefore, they can be pronounced either true or false, and be either contrary or conformable to reason.'[2]

It is precisely from this point that his criticism of Wollaston begins. And he is fully aware that this consideration affects our moral feelings and such actions as may flow from them, exactly as it affects all other feelings and actions; and that it would be a lapse into an error like Wollaston's to treat our moral reactions as exhausted in such feelings and actions (i.e. as including no distinctively moral *judgements*), and at the same time as being capable of truth and falsehood. Nor is he guilty of any such lapse himself. But the same cannot be said of his friend Adam Smith, nor of some of his spiritual descendants at the present time.

Smith's account of the 'propriety' of emotions and actions,

[1] *Treatise*, II. iii. 3.   [2] III. i. I.

i.e. of their 'moral appropriateness' to their circumstances, is in some ways more subtle than Hume's, though it is of the same general sort. 'To approve of the passions of another . . . as suitable to their objects,' Smith holds, 'is the same thing as to observe that we entirely sympathise with them; and not to approve of them as such, is the same thing as to observe that we do not entirely sympathise with them.'[1] This reference to the 'objects' provoking the 'passions' is not merely ornamental; for what Smith calls 'sympathy' with the emotions of another, i.e. sharing them, does not, in his opinion, 'arise so much from the view of the passion, as from that of the situation which excites it'.[2] We do not automatically share the feelings we observe in another; but we automatically 'put ourselves in his place', and envisage what we would feel if his situation were ours. If we then find that his actual emotion or action is what we ourselves would have felt or done in his situation, we are pleased with this harmony between our ways of reacting, and express this pleasure by calling his reaction a 'proper' one. There is at this point a minor ambiguity analogous to that which we have noticed in Hume. In the definition of 'approval' just quoted, Smith identifies it with the *perception* that another's reaction is what ours would have been in his place ('to approve . . . is the same thing as to observe. . . .'); but he often speaks as if it were identical rather with the *pleasure* which we take in this perception. This, however, in Smith as in Hume, is a minor point; what is important is that the only judgement involved in moral approval is, on Smith's view, one about the speaker's feelings—not exactly the judgement that the observed reaction gives the speaker an agreeable feeling, but that it coincides with what he would have felt, or felt like doing, in similar circumstances.

Smith also describes a more complex and important kind of 'moral sentiment' which arises when we consider not only

---

[1] *Theory of Moral Sentiments*, I. i. 3.   [2] I. i. 1.

the situation of the person whose reaction we are judging but also the situation in which his reaction places other people. If a man's reaction is 'proper', in the sense just indicated, and also places others in a situation in which we would feel gratitude, then the reaction has, in our eyes, not only propriety but 'merit'. Correspondingly, if an 'improper' reaction (i.e. one which we cannot imagine as having been our own) places others in a situation in which we would feel resentment, it has not only impropriety but demerit or blameworthiness. Mr. Carritt, in a recent comment on Smith, seems to misinterpret him at this point. He begins by noting the subjectivism implicit in the equation of what *is* 'proper' with what *seems* to suit the situation, when Smith writes, 'In the suitableness or unsuitableness, in the proportion or disproportion which the affection *seems* to bear to the cause or object which excites it, consists the propriety or impropriety, the decency or ungracefulness of the consequent action.'[1] But he sees an 'inconsequent' transition to a more objective view in the account of merit and demerit which immediately follows: 'In the beneficial or hurtful nature of the effects which the affection aims at, or tends to produce, consists the merit or demerit of the action, the qualities by which it is entitled to reward, or is deserving of punishment.' It is true that this is objectivist language—it seems to identify the merit or demerit of the action with a tendency in the action itself, or in the 'affection' giving rise to it, and not with anything merely 'in the eye of the beholder'. But the key words are 'beneficial' and 'hurtful', and Smith makes it quite clear that the distinction between these qualities does depend on the emotional constitution of the man who is making it.

'When I hear of a benefit that has been bestowed upon another person, let him who has received it be affected in what manner he pleases, if, by bringing his case home to myself, I feel gratitude arise

---

[1] *Theory of Moral Sentiments*, I. i. 3, quoted in *Ethical and Political Thinking*, p. 41; italics Mr. Carritt's.

in my own breast, I necessarily approve of the conduct of his bene-factor, and regard it as meritorious, and the proper object of reward.'[1]

Here, as in the other case, the ultimate judgement depends on the feelings of the beholder. The notion of merit is, in fact, so far from differing in this respect from the notion of propriety, that it is, in Smith's system, derived from this very notion of propriety. The derivation is evident in the con-cluding words of the passage just quoted. An act is meri-torious if, and only if, it would be 'proper' to reward it—that is, if we could 'sympathize' with anyone who did reward it, because we would ourselves be inclined to reward it had we been the persons affected by it.

There is so little of naïve inconsequence in Smith's distinc-tion between propriety and merit that it enables him to give an exceedingly sophisticated—and exceedingly modern—solution of the question as to whether we approve of any-thing but the promotion of pleasure and the prevention of pain. He holds that the acute differences of opinion which have arisen on this point are due to a failure to realize that the term 'approve' is ambiguous. The 'sense of propriety and impropriety' is called into play independently of the bene-ficial or hurtful effects of the acts and dispositions we are contemplating; and this sense of propriety and impropriety is a necessary ingredient in all forms of approval and dis-approval; but beneficent and maleficent actions, and benevo-lent and malevolent dispositions, stand out from all others as the objects of that more complicated form of approval and disapproval which Smith calls the sense of merit and demerit. Systems which place all virtue in propriety do not 'account either easily or sufficiently for that superior degree of esteem which seems due' to beneficent actions, or for the 'superior degree of detestation' with which we regard 'deliberate actions, of a pernicious tendency to those we live with'.[2] On the other hand, systems which place all virtue in benevolence, 'have

---

[1] *Theory of Moral Sentiments*, II. i. 5, concluding note.   [2] VII. ii. I.

the contrary defect, of not sufficiently explaining . . . our approbation of the inferior virtues of prudence, vigilance, circumspection, temperance, constancy, firmness'.[1]

There is one point, however, at which Smith is guilty of serious confusion, and that is where he puts forward a thoroughgoing parallelism between our judgement as to the propriety or impropriety of a man's response to his situation, and our judgement as to the truth or falsehood of his opinion.

'To approve of another man's opinions is to adopt those opinions, and to adopt them is to approve of them. If the same arguments which convince you, convince me likewise, I necessarily approve of your conviction; and if they do not, I necessarily disapprove of it; neither can I possibly conceive that I should do the one without the other. To approve or disapprove, therefore, of the opinions of others is acknowledged, by everybody, to mean no more than to observe their agreement or disagreement with our own. But this is equally the case with regard to our approbation or disapprobation of the sentiments or passions of others. . . . Every faculty in one man is the measure by which he judges of the like faculty in another. I judge of your sight by my sight, of your ear by my ear, of your reason by my reason, of your resentment by my resentment, of your love by my love. I neither have, nor can have, any other way of judging about them.'[2]

The trouble with this argument is, of course, that it is *not* 'acknowledged by everybody'—it is not acknowledged, for example, by either Reid or Hume—that 'to approve or disapprove of the opinions of others' *means* no more than 'to observe their agreement or disagreement with our own'. It would probably be acknowledged that we would in fact approve of all opinions coinciding with our own, and of no others; but *why* would we? Plainly, many would say, because to make an opinion 'our own' is to regard it as true, i.e. as a perception or representation of a fact beyond the opinion itself; and it is because of the supposed accordance of

---

[1] *Theory of Moral Sentiments*, VII. ii. 3.   [2] I. i. 3.

another man's opinion with this fact, rather than because of its known accordance with our own opinion, that we approve of it, i.e. consider it true. We can always envisage the possibility that although we consider the other man's opinion to be true, it may not be so in fact, because our own may not be so either. The coincidence of another man's opinion with ours we take to be a sign of its truth, but we do not identify this coincidence with its truth. On the other hand, Smith does identify the 'propriety' of another man's feeling with its coincidence with our own. The supposed analogy between such propriety and the truth of an opinion therefore disappears.

It should be added that although Smith has at this point introduced a confusion which is quite absent from Hume's account of our moral consciousness, the confusion probably has its roots in Hume's more general theory of knowledge, and particularly in his theory of belief or opinion.[1] Here Hume says that 'the vulgar division of the acts of the understanding into *conception, judgment* and *reasoning*' is erroneous, and that 'taking them in a proper light', all three 'resolve themselves into the first, and are nothing but particular ways of conceiving our objects'.[2] A belief or opinion, i.e. a judgement, is simply a conception or idea which happens to have greater 'force and vivacity' than fictitious ones; and a completely certain belief, e.g. the belief that I am having a certain feeling, would on this view be identical with what Hume calls an 'impression', in this case with the feeling that I am having. No doubt Hume's formal adherence to this ridiculous theory accounts for his indifference to the distinction between the feeling of approval and the judgement that we have such a feeling, but in his detailed handling of the relation between feeling and judgement in the moral consciousness the theory is simply abandoned, and the logical strength of his discussion of this relation results entirely from its abandonment.

[1] *Treatise*, i. iii. 7; *Enquiry concerning Human Understanding*, v. ii.
[2] *Treatise*, i. iii. 7.

VII

PROPRIETY AND TRUTH:
(2) FACTS AND NORMS

AMONG Hume's present-day followers there is not the uncertainty which we find in Hume himself as to whether a moral judgement is to be identified with the judgement that an object is evoking in us a feeling of approval or disapproval, or with that feeling itself. They are very emphatic in taking the latter line, having been convinced of the unplausibility of the former identification by an argument of Professor Moore's. And they have accepted most of the consequences of this position to which Reid drew attention; but not quite all. They agree that the verbal expression of a so-called ethical judgement, since it is not properly so called, is not properly speaking a proposition, and is not capable of truth or falsehood; though they do not agree that these 'pseudo-propositions' of Ethics have literally no meaning. 'Such a man did well and worthily', they would hold, has the same meaning as an exclamation—'How pleasing is that deed!', or 'Hurrah for him!'—or a command—'Go and do thou likewise.' This school has found its most forceful spokesman in Professor A. J. Ayer.[1] Mr. Carritt argues that such forms of speech as commands and exclamations, addressed to other people, will not be understood unless they convey the information that the person uttering them wants something to be done, or is pleased or displeased.[2] I am not sure that this is actually the case. When a person says 'Shut the door!' I think another person might shut it without reflecting even for an instant that the first one wants it shut; and even if 'Shut the door!' does mean, among other things, 'I want you to shut the door', the command has a further purpose, over and above

[1] *Language, Truth and Logic*, ch. vi.
[2] *Ethical and Political Thinking*, p. 32 (see Note A, p. 108).

the conveying of this information, which cannot be expressed in strictly propositional form, and yet may reasonably be called part of the 'meaning' of the utterance.

Not all, however, of those who thus identify ethical propositions, not with statements about, but with expressions of, feelings and desires, are as fully prepared as Professor Ayer is to accept what seem to be the plain consequences of such a position. Some, while agreeing that such expressions are not capable of truth or falsehood, argue, like Smith, that they are capable of something very like them; others go so far as to regard them as capable of truth and falsehood themselves. To the first class belongs Dr. K. R. Popper; to the second, Professor J. N. Findlay. I shall consider Dr. Popper's view in the remainder of the present study and Professor Findlay's in the next.

Dr. Popper insists as strongly as any writer of the modern subjectivist school upon the 'non-descriptive' character of ethical precepts. Such precepts do not express facts, but either are or express (it is not clear which) what Dr. Popper calls 'norms'; and they are not deducible from sentences expressing facts, not even from sentences expressing the fact that a norm is, as Dr. Popper puts it, 'agreed with' by some person or society. 'That most people agree with the norm "Thou shalt not steal" is a sociological fact. But the norm "Thou shalt not steal" is not a fact; and it can never be inferred from sentences describing facts.' To make the point quite clear, the relation between the norm expressed by 'Thou shalt not steal' and the fact that most people 'agree' with it is compared with the relation between the fact that Napoleon died on St. Helena and the fact that a certain Mr. A says that he did; we cannot infer the norm expressed by 'Thou shalt not steal' from the fact that most people 'agree' with it, any more than we can infer that Napoleon died on St. Helena from the fact that Mr. A says so.[1]

[1] *The Open Society and its Enemies*, vol. i, p. 53.

What all this suggests is that a 'norm' may be described as 'that which is expressed by a command' (for I take it that 'Thou shalt not steal' means 'Don't steal' rather than 'You are not going to steal', since the latter would undoubtedly count as a 'sentence describing a fact'). And there is a further suggestion that a norm is what a command expresses, not in the sense in which a proposition expresses a *judgement*, but in the sense in which a proposition, or at all events a true proposition, expresses a *fact*. It is not the internal thing to which a command gives voice, as a sentence gives voice to a judgement (this, in the case of a command, would be a desire, or as Dr. Popper says, a 'decision', that something should be done), but the external thing to which a command refers. Now the common view about this is that there is just no such thing—that although particular words in a command may refer to objects, as particular words in a sentence may do, there is nothing to which the command itself refers, as the sentence itself refers to a fact. The 'meaning' of commands, as it is sometimes said, is purely 'expressive', and not 'referential'. But with this point of view Dr. Popper does not agree. He will not have it that 'the reason why norms cannot be derived from factual propositions is that norms are meaningless'; and that, for him, 'expressive' meaning is not enough, is indicated by his dismissing as 'psychologism' the view that norms are 'habits'. 'The reluctance to admit that norms are something important and irreducible', he goes on to say, 'is one of the main sources of the intellectual and other weaknesses of the progressive circles of our time.'[1] And as if to emphasize the objectivity of 'norms' still more heavily, he then says that there is one sort of fact from which they *can* be inferred.

In leading up to this point, he remarks that although we cannot infer that Napoleon died on St. Helena from the fact that Mr. A says so, if the latter fact is taken on its own, we

[1] p. 204.

can do so if it is conjoined with the fact that what Mr. A says is true. And he suggests that in 'the realm of norms' we might 'introduce, in correspondence with the concept of truth, the concept of the *validity* of a norm. This would mean that a certain norm *N* could be derived . . . from a sentence stating that *N* is valid. And . . . if we use the word "fact" in such a wide sense that we speak of *the fact that a norm is valid*, then we could even derive norms from facts.'[1] I suspect that the wording of this is a little careless. Dr. Popper classifies 'the fact that a norm is valid' along with 'the fact that a sentence is true' as 'semantic' facts, i.e. facts concerning the relations between expressions and what they mean. A sentence is true when what it asserts is a fact; and the 'semantic' fact about norms which corresponds with this would have to be a fact about the relation between the *expression* of a norm and the norm itself. It would be more accurate, I should say, to speak of a *command* as being valid when what it commands is a norm, so that we can infer the norm, *Thou shalt not steal*, from the fact that the command not to steal is valid, as we can infer the fact, *Napoleon died on St. Helena*, from the fact that the statement that he did so is true. And again, just as we can infer 'Napoleon died on St. Helena' from 'Mr. A states that Napoleon died on St. Helena, and Mr. A's statement is true', so we can infer 'Don't steal!' from 'Mr. A forbids stealing, and Mr. A's prohibition is valid'.

But just what is this 'validity' which commands and prohibitions may or may not possess? Although commands and prohibitions cannot be true or false, there is at least one relational property which they do possess, which presents many formal analogies with truth and falsehood, and that is the property of being obeyed or disobeyed.[2] The truth or falsehood of a proposition depends on something completely outside itself, namely, a fact, and we cannot normally tell whether a proposition is true or false by merely inspecting

[1] p. 205.   [2] see Note B, p. 108.

the proposition itself. Similarly, a command's being obeyed or disobeyed depends on something completely outside itself, namely, what is actually done by those to whom it is addressed; and we cannot normally tell whether a command will be obeyed or not merely by inspecting the command itself. With propositions there is an exception in the case of tautologies and contradictions—we can see that 'What is human is human' is true, and that 'Something human is not human' is false, without having to refer to any fact beyond the propositions themselves. Correspondingly, we can see that the command 'Do what you will do' will be obeyed, and that 'Do what you will not do' will be disobeyed, without having to refer to any deed beyond the command itself. And corresponding in a similar way to the truth and falsehood of judgements is the satisfaction and frustration of desires. We might suppose, therefore, that 'Mr. A's prohibition is valid' simply means 'What Mr. A forbids, does not occur'. But all that this enables us to infer from 'Mr. A forbids us to steal' is 'Stealing does not occur'; and this, if it is the case, is certainly to be classed as a fact, and therefore not as a 'norm'.

Before making another suggestion, it may be useful to refer to the way in which Adam Smith dealt with a somewhat similar problem. Smith, like Hume, was a student and disciple of Hutcheson; but not an uncritical one. He was impressed with Hutcheson's proofs that approval and disapproval were not judgements of reason but the work of 'immediate sense and feeling'; but he could not agree that the 'moral sense' was something *sui generis*—it was to provide an alternative to this that he produced his own elaborate derivation of approval and disapproval from 'sympathy'. And one of his objections to Hutcheson's view was that it made it senseless to talk of approving and disapproving of the moral sense itself. For the qualities which a given sense perceives cannot be ascribed without absurdity to the sense itself. 'Who ever thought of calling the sense of seeing, black or white;

the sense of hearing, loud or low; or the sense of tasting, sweet or bitter? And, according to him'—i.e. Hutcheson—'it is equally absurd to call our moral faculties virtuous or vicious, morally good or evil.' To Smith this conclusion was quite intolerable.

'Surely, if we saw any man shouting with admiration and applause at a barbarous and unmerited execution which some insolent tyrant had ordered, we should not think we were guilty of any great absurdity in denominating this behaviour vicious and morally evil in the greatest degree, though it expressed nothing but depraved moral faculties, or an absurd approbation of this horrid action, as of what was noble, magnanimous and great.'

Conversely, 'correct moral sentiments appear in some degree laudable and morally good'. Smith, it is plain, was concerned to establish something very like a distinction between valid and invalid norms.

At first glance it may appear that what Smith was complaining of in Hutcheson was an excess of subjectivism. But in fact it was precisely the element of objectivism or rationalism in Hutcheson which involved him in the conclusion to which Smith objected. For anyone who regards moral approbation as a perception that an object possesses a certain real character, whether this perception be the work of reason or of a sense, is bound to regard the approbation itself as beyond praise or blame. We cannot blame a man for a mistaken judgement (though we can blame him for not trying hard enough to arrive at a true one); of such a judgement all we can say is that it is mistaken, not that it is morally bad. It is only if we regard approbation, not as a judgement about an emotional response, but as an emotional response to another emotional response, that we can think of it as itself a possible object of approbation; for this last would then merely mean, thinking of it as itself possibly evoking an emotional response. And that the subjectivism, in this controversy, was all on

Smith's side is quite plain from his positive account of how we approve or disapprove of another's approval.

'How is it that . . . we approve or disapprove of proper or improper approbation? To this question there is, I imagine, but one reasonable answer that can be given. It must be said, that when the approbation with which our neighbour regards the conduct of a third person coincides with our own, we approve of his approbation, and consider it as in some measure morally good; and that, on the contrary, when it does not coincide with our own sentiments, we disapprove of it, and consider it as in some measure morally bad.'[1]

The propriety of approval is not finally determined, any more than the propriety of any other emotional response is finally determined, by the character of the situation evoking it; it depends, as all other propriety depends, on the emotional response of the person *to whom* it is proper. Propriety, we may say, is on this system always propriety *to* someone; and this applies to the propriety of approval as much as to that of anything else. The notion of the propriety of a 'judgement of propriety', in other words, does not take us one single step towards the notion of the truth of a 'judgement of propriety', or towards the notion of an absolute or 'factual' propriety, a propriety which could be possessed by responses considered in themselves, or only in relation to the situation evoking them.

Now it seems to me that the notion of the 'validity of a norm' will only do the work which Dr. Popper wants to make it do, if we regard it as something analogous to Smith's 'propriety of an approbation'. For it seems to me perfectly clear that if 'Mr. A's prohibition is valid' is going to enable us to infer 'Don't steal' from 'Mr. A forbids us to steal', there is one thing and one thing only which it can possibly mean; and that is: 'What Mr. A forbids, don't do.' And if 'Don't steal' cannot describe a fact, then this cannot describe a fact

[1] *Theory of Moral Sentiments*, Part VII, Sect. iii, ch. iii.

either. If it describes or refers to anything at all, i.e. if its meaning is not merely 'expressive', what it describes or refers to is a 'second-order norm'. At the same time, on this interpretation of 'Mr. A's prohibition is valid', such utterances give us no reason whatever to believe that there *are* such things as 'norms', distinct both from commands and from the desires (or decisions, or habits) which commands express, and conferring validity on both in the same way as facts confer truth on propositions and judgements. For since such utterances, on this interpretation, are themselves commands and prohibitions, they do not take us one single step towards seeing how commands and prohibitions can have something like the factual reference of affirmations and negations. 'Don't do what Mr. A forbids' no doubt expresses our endorsement of Mr. A's prohibition; but this only means that it expresses our desire that his desires should be satisfied (it expresses the propriety, to us, of his prohibition, in Smith's wholly subjective sense of 'propriety'). It is not at all like our 'endorsement' of another man's statements or opinions, which always has behind it the idea that those statements or opinions accord, not merely with our own opinions, but with the facts with which we regard our own opinions as according also.

An ethical rationalist, of course, can give to such a statement as 'Mr. A's prohibition is valid' a perfectly straightforward meaning, namely, 'What Mr. A forbids, we ought not to do.' From this, together with 'Mr. A forbids us to steal', we can infer 'We ought not to steal'. On this interpretation, however, what the conclusion refers to is at least as truly a fact as the fact that we ought not to do what Mr. A forbids—that is, it is at least as truly a fact as the fact that Mr. A's prohibition is valid. So that if what Dr. Popper means by a 'norm' is (as one cannot help sometimes suspecting it is) what is referred to by such expressions as 'We ought not to steal', his distinction between norms and facts breaks down. What also breaks down, if we interpret 'validity'[1] in this way, is the analogy between 'validity' and truth. For what the notion of the truth of a person's statements enables us to do is to pass from the assertion that the person says 'X is the case' to the independent assertion that X *is* the case. Now on the interpretation of 'validity' that we are now considering, it does not enable us to pass from the assertion that a person utters the prohibition 'Don't steal' to the independent utterance of this same prohibition; what it enables us to do is rather to pass from the assertion that the person utters the prohibition 'Don't steal', to something that is not a mere prohibition at all, but an assertion of an objective obligation— 'We ought not to steal'; or 'Stealing is wrong'. We could, of course, bring 'truth' into it if we used the inference 'Mr. A says that we ought not to steal; and what Mr. A says is true; therefore we ought not to steal'. But in this case, our first premiss is not that Mr. A utters a prohibition, but that he makes a statement; and our second premiss is not that his prohibition has something *like* truth, namely, 'validity', but that his statement has 'truth' itself; and the whole thing, like Wollaston's attempted reduction of 'rightness' to 'truth', does not 'explain' obligation, but presupposes it.

[1] See Note C, p. 109.

VIII

PROPRIETY AND TRUTH:
(3) FEELINGS AND CLAIMS

Professor Findlay, in a very important article which appeared a few years ago,[1] begins by squarely taking his place with the 'writers of the sentimental school in the eighteenth century'. Referring to the usual set of ethical predicates—'good', 'bad', 'right', 'wrong', 'ought', &c.—he says that 'a man who . . . uses some of these peculiar words, is not, while he uses them, trying to "discover objects as they stand in nature, without addition or diminution"; he is rather trying to give voice to the demands and feelings which the notion of such objects arouses in him'.[2] The phrase 'give voice to' is important. 'The modern sentimentalist' is superior to his eighteenth-century forbears in being 'quite clear that, if we say: "This thing is good", "This should be done" and so forth, we are not talking *of* our own demands and feelings, but rather *giving voice* to them. Whereas the doctrines of the earlier sentimentalists leave it vague whether they think the moral judgment *voices* sentiment, or merely *talks about* it.'[3] There are, however, certain 'modern' ways of speaking which Professor Findlay thinks are anything but an improvement upon the old. He considers it 'bizarre and curious' to say, as many contemporary writers do, 'that moral judgments are not really judgements, that they do not express propositions capable of truth and falsehood, and that they are wholly lacking in "factual content"'. 'These statements', he admits, may be valuable in 'bringing out the difference between a moral judgement, which gives voice to an attitude, and other judgements which we should describe as "factual" in a narrow sense'.

---

[1] 'Morality by Convention', in *Mind*, 1944.
[2] p. 143.   [3] pp. 145–6.

'But it is altogether arbitrary, and also contrary to accepted usage, to say that what we *call* moral judgements have not, in strictness, any right to be classed as judgements. And it is also wholly arbitrary to deny the right of certain judgements to be denominated "true" and "valid". For, as we shall make it our business to show, there is a whole gamut of tests to which a moral judgement, just *because* it is a moral judgement, must necessarily submit itself: it is customary and proper to say of judgements that survive these tests that they are true or valid.'[1]

Professor Findlay's main concern is, of course, to show that distinctively ethical desires and demands, and the expressions which 'voice' them, are like judgements and propositions in being capable of truth and falsehood; but he prepares the way for this demonstration by arguing that, if not the same thing, at all events something very like it, may be said of desires and demands, or 'emotions', quite generally. He particularly emphasizes the fact that

'even in the case of the most familiar and elementary emotions, we find . . . certain definite *claims* involved in them, whose validation would serve to *justify* a man in feeling them. Thus in the emotion that we call "fear" we see some object "in a menacing light"; it must seem dangerous, a source of possible harm; we couldn't be afraid of something that was *obviously* harmless. And it is plain that, if an object was really harmless, our fears of it would forthwith *lose their justification*. And it is plain that, if we *knew* an object wasn't really harmful, and nevertheless continued to fear it, our fear would rightly be denominated "neurotic" or "abnormal". To be afraid of objects therefore means, in part, to treat them as having certain properties, to make a claim with regard to them, a claim which may be true or false, whose verification will serve to justify our frightened state, and whose refutation will altogether remove this justification. . . . It would be possible, in a similar fashion, to show that jealousy and anger . . . make various complicated claims regarding actual situations, and that they immediately lose their justification if any of these claims should prove unfounded.'[2]

[1] pp. 146–7.   [2] pp. 147–8.

The same point is made in a later article by the same writer, on a connected subject. 'All attitudes'—and he means, primarily, emotional attitudes—'*presume* characters in their objects, and are, in consequence, strengthened by the discovery that their objects *have* these characters, as they are weakened by the discovery that they haven't got them.'[1]

What Professor Findlay means by this language—by speaking of emotions as making or involving 'claims', and of attitudes as 'presuming' certain things—seems clear enough, and true enough. Our emotions and attitudes depend on what we believe to be the case; they depend, that is to say, on our implicit or explicit judgements; and if those judgements are altered, our emotions are liable to alter also. And in view of this dependence of emotions on judgements, we may call an emotion or attitude 'unjustified' if it depends on a judgement that is false—i.e. if we would not have had it but for this false judgement. Correspondingly, we may call an emotion or attitude 'justified' if the judgement on which it depends happens to be a true one. We may go farther, and transfer the epithet 'true' or 'false' to the emotion itself, or to the emotion and the judgement considered as a single complex state of mind. This is, indeed, a rather peculiar use of the terms 'true' and 'false', but it is not without parallels. Consider, for example, the judgement which a man might express by saying 'That tiger has purple eyes'. We would call this judgement false—in the ordinary sense of 'false'— if and only if the tiger in question *hadn't* purple eyes. But we might also call it false—in a slightly queer sense of 'false'—if there were no tiger there. So why should we not also apply the term 'false' to the expression (or to the state of mind voiced by the expression) 'Mind that tiger!' if there were no tiger there?

It should not be overlooked, however, that this criterion gives us no means of distinguishing, as regards their 'truth'

[1] 'Can God's Existence be Disproved?', in *Mind,* 1948, p. 178.

and 'falsehood', between the states of mind voiced by the two expressions 'Mind that tiger!' and 'Never mind that tiger!' Either expression might be seriously uttered by a person who fully believed in the reality of the tiger (though the second reaction would certainly be unusual); and this is the plane on which ethical disagreement occurs, on any 'emotive' view of our ethical responses. No amount of juggling with unusual senses of 'true' and 'false' can do away with this difference between judgements and emotions: The truth or falsehood of a judgement that a certain object has a certain character depends on whether the object in fact has or has not that character, and on nothing else whatever. On the other hand, what emotion we feel towards an object never depends solely on what its character is, or even what we believe it to be, but always in part on how we ourselves are constituted—on what characters produce what emotions *in us*. The suggested way of talking, in other words, in no way alters the fact that an emotion which is 'true' for one person, i.e. is what he would feel if he knew the facts, may be 'false' for another, i.e. may not be what *he* would feel if he knew the facts; whereas judgements are *not* in this way 'true' for one person and 'false' for another.

Professor Findlay's point about judgements being implicit in emotions is not by any means a new one; it was raised, for instance, by Hume, whose treatment of it seems to me completely adequate.

'As nothing can be contrary to truth or reason, except what has a reference to it, and as the judgments of our understanding only have this reference, it must follow that passions can be contrary to reason only, so far as they are *accompanied* with some judgment or opinion. According to this principle, . . . it is only in two senses that any affection can be called unreasonable. First, when a passion, such as hope or fear, grief or joy, despair or security, is founded on the supposition of objects, which really do not exist. Secondly, when in exerting any passion in action, we choose means insufficient for the designed end, and deceive ourselves in our judgment of causes and effects. Where a passion is neither founded on false suppositions, nor chooses means insufficient for the end, the understanding can neither justify nor condemn it. It is not contrary to reason to prefer the destruction of the whole world to the scratching of my finger. It is not contrary to reason for me to choose my total ruin, to prevent the least uneasiness of an Indian, or person wholly unknown to me. . . . In short, a passion must be accompanied with some false judgment, in order to its being unreasonable; and even then it is not the passion, properly speaking, which is unreasonable, but the judgment.'[1]

The same line of reasoning is extended to actions, though here the matter is a little more complicated. An action, according to Hume, cannot arise directly from a judgement, but it may arise from an emotion or desire 'founded on' a judgement, in the sense above indicated; and it may not only arise from a judgement, in this indirect way, but may also, in another indirect way which we shall discuss shortly, be the cause of judgements in others. But as in the case of emotion, 'though no will or action can be immediately contradictory to reason, yet we may find such a contradiction in some of the attendants of the action . . .; and by an abusive way of speaking, which philosophy will scarce allow of, the same contrariety may, upon that account, be ascribed to the action'.[2]

An ethical rationalist might, of course, call an emotion or action 'reasonable' when it is 'such as our reason discerns to be right'. Price, for example, gives this as the meaning of the phrase 'conformity of our actions to reason', though he notes that as a method of 'explaining virtue' this phrase is useless—we can only talk in this way if we believe that 'rightness' and 'wrongness' cannot be 'explained' at all.[3] And a man who talks like this might hold, in particular, that it is proper or

---

[1] *Treatise*, II. iii. 3.   [2] III. i. 1.
[3] *Review*, ch. vi; Selby-Bigge, 694.

G

right (and so 'reasonable') to be pleased with what we judge to be good, and displeased with what we judge to be bad. The 'reasonableness' of the approval felt towards, say, generosity, would then be, as it were, a double reasonableness—such approval would be reasonable, firstly because it is reasonable, i.e. right or proper, to be pleased with what we judge to be morally good; and secondly because the judgement that generosity is morally good is reasonable, i.e. true. Reid, for example, held that approval was thus complex, and that the emotional element in it presupposed, or as Professor Findlay would say 'presumed', or 'involved the claim', that the object approved of was good; though he over-simplified matters by substituting for the 'propriety' of feeling pleased with goodness, a sort of natural inevitability that we should do so. 'When I see a man exerting himself nobly in a good cause . . . I am conscious that the effect of his conduct on my mind is *complex*, though it may be called by *one name*, I look up to his virtue, I approve, I admire it. In doing so, I have pleasure indeed, or an agreeable feeling.' But this 'agreeable feeling' is entirely dependent 'upon *the judgment I form of his conduct*. I judge that this conduct merits esteem; and, while I thus judge, I cannot but esteem him, and contemplate his conduct with pleasure. Persuade me . . . that he acted from some . . . bad motive, immediately my esteem and my agreeable feeling vanish.'[1] Reid could not accept Hume's account of virtue as conduct or character which we find it agreeable to contemplate, because for him the particular sort of agreeable feeling which the contemplation of virtue evoked depended on the prior judgement that it *was* virtue that was being contemplated. As Sidgwick later put it:

'The peculiar emotion of moral approbation is, in my experience, inseparably bound up with the conviction, implicit or explicit, that the conduct approved is "really" right. . . . So far, then, from being prepared to admit that the proposition "X ought

[1] *Essays on the Active Powers*, v. vii.

to be done" *merely* expresses the existence of a certain sentiment in myself or in others, I find it strictly impossible so to regard my own moral judgments without eliminating from the concomitant sentiment the peculiar quality signified by the term "moral".[1]

Hume agreed that the pleasure or displeasure taken by men in the conduct and character which they observed would depend in part on what sort of conduct and character they judged it to be (there are some kinds of it that a man likes, some that he does not); but he could not without a somewhat Wollastonian circularity have included the judgement that the conduct or character was good or bad among those thus influencing men's emotional response to it, since he defined goodness and badness in terms of the emotional response itself. (To say that our liking or disliking of it depended on its goodness or badness would be, on his view, to say that our liking or disliking of it depended on our liking or disliking of it.) Nor, of course, did he attempt to include such judgements among those presupposed by approval and disapproval—he knew quite well that this was where he and the ethical rationalists parted company. He says explicitly that although 'false judgments may be thought to affect the passions and actions, which are connected with them, and may be said to render them unreasonable, in a figurative and improper way of speaking', nevertheless such errors 'extend not beyond a matter of *fact*, which moralists have not generally supposed criminal'. Professor Findlay also knows that this is where an ethical rationalist and a disciple of Hume must part company; but he is more persistent than his master in attempting to justify the formulation of a sentimentalist or subjectivist theory in rationalist language.

Sometimes we describe a response to a situation as 'unjustified' or 'unreasonable' when it is unusual. One reason why unusual responses may be called 'unreasonable', or even 'untrue', is that, as Hume points out, they are likely to lead

[1] *Methods of Ethics*, I. iii. 1–2.

those who perceive the response, but not the situation evoking it, to form false conclusions as to what the situation is. One possible meaning of Wollaston's contention that 'a man that is ungrateful to his benefactor . . . affirms that he never received any favours from him', is that 'human nature is generally grateful, and makes us conclude that a man who does any harm, never receives any favour from the person he harmed'. The action thus 'causes . . . a mistake and false judgement by accident; and the falsehood of its effects may be ascribed, by some odd figurative way of speaking, to the action itself'.[1] The mistake is caused 'by accident'; for the false conclusion does not follow from the action itself, or from the fact that it has occurred (no fact can entail a falsehood); but from the fact conjoined with the mistaken belief that the action is a response to the sort of situation which *usually* evokes it. And since the action itself is not in the least responsible for this mistaken belief, it seems a little hard to transfer to it the 'falsehood' of the conclusion to which the belief gives rise.[2]

Professor Findlay treats 'abnormal' or unusual ethical responses as 'false' for almost but not quite this reason. It is not so much that they mislead others, as that they presuppose a certain *self*-deception or false judgement. For an ethical response—Professor Findlay makes this a matter of definition —is one made in the belief that it is *not* unusual; it is one which we demand that others share with us, and which we also expect that others will share with us. And if this expectation is unrealized—if we find that we have misjudged what the responses of others will be—a response of the sort which Professor Findlay calls 'ethical' will weaken or alter; while if it is realized, it will become stronger and more stable. The 'others' to whom we thus appeal are not, however, just *any* others. We appeal only to those who have duly 'reflected' on the conduct of which we are approving or disapproving, or

---

[1] *Treatise*, III. i. 1.   [2] See Note D, p. 109.

on what we feel like doing or not doing—to those who have given 'careful scrutiny' to all its aspects and effects and evoking circumstances, and have entered imaginatively into the situation of all whom the conduct in question concerns.

'We make our appeal above the unreflective heads of "present company", to the "great company of reflective persons", wherever they may be situated in space or time. . . . But we should not be speaking ethically at all, if we were not making our appeal to some such company, if we were not submitting our immediate, primary attitude to some such form of social testing. And since we look for agreement on the part of all reflective persons, it follows that our moral attitudes will become more confident whenever we find such persons in agreement with us, and that they will, in a similar manner, be weakened and discredited whenever such persons cast their vote against us.'[1]

We appeal, also, to the results of fuller 'reflection' on our own part—an ethical response is one involving a claim that it will not be altered by further consideration of the case (it is as if we said, 'How I dislike what he has done!—nothing will make me like it'); and if such further consideration does alter it, we may say that the original response was 'unjustified', 'invalid', or 'untrue'.[2] The process of reflection must include, further, a careful attempt to distinguish from our ethical response any emotions arising from our own personal interest in the action being judged. Ethical responses—this also is simply a matter of definition—claim to be impartial; and this is the most essential thing about them.[3] We naturally take pleasure, for instance, in another's kindness to ourselves; but of this pleasure, only that portion is to count as 'moral approval' which we would also have taken in his kindness to anyone else in the like circumstances.

In all this there are clear and conscious echoes of Hume; but some differences too. To Professor Findlay's doctrine that an ethical response claims to be capable of withstanding

[1] *Mind*, 1944, p. 160.   [2] p. 158.   [3] pp. 161–2.

reflective consideration corresponds Hume's that the final judgement of praise or blame can only be passed 'after every circumstance, every relation is known'. The disinterestedness or impartiality of moral emotion is stressed by Hume too. Not every 'sentiment of pleasure or pain, which arises from characters and actions', is of 'that *peculiar* kind which makes us praise or condemn. The good qualities of an enemy are hurtful to us, but may still command our esteem and respect. It is only when a character is considered in general, without reference to our particular interest, that it causes such a feeling or sentiment as denominates it morally good or evil'.[1] This point, as Professor Findlay notes, was very fully developed by Adam Smith; we shall glance at what he made of it shortly.

Hume is also sometimes credited with the view that 'X is good' means not so much that X gives the speaker a feeling of approval, as that it gives such a feeling to everyone, or almost everyone. He is thus interpreted, for example, in a much-criticized passage in Professor Broad's *Five Types of Ethical Theory*.[2] The logical consequence of such a view, Professor Broad points out, 'is not that in disputes on moral questions there comes a point beyond which we can only say "*de gustibus non disputandum*"', but that 'all such disputes *could* be settled, and that the way to settle them is to collect statistics of how people in fact do feel. And to me', he adds, 'this kind of answer seems utterly irrelevant to this kind of question.'[3] Professor Findlay's view that we 'expect' others to agree with our ethical responses looks very like an attempt to put the theory here criticized into a form in which it is defensible; but it is questionable whether in any case the theory is justly attributed to Hume. Hume does say, indeed, that 'amidst all the variety and caprice of taste, there are certain general principles of approbation or blame, whose influence a careful eye may trace in all the operations of the

[1] *Treatise*, III. i. 2.   [2] pp. 85–6.   [3] p. 115.

mind. Some particular forms or qualities, from the original structure of the internal fabric, are calculated to please, and others to displease.'[1] This is said of 'taste' generally; but it is no doubt meant to apply to 'moral taste' in particular. And in the *Enquiry concerning the Principles of Morals* Hume sets out to summarize and systematize the qualities which evoke approval and disapproval in men generally. But I do not think his aim here is to arrive at a standard by which the moral reactions of individuals may be corrected; what he seeks, rather, is a generalization suggesting how they may be explained. And I do not think he means to define approval and disapproval as reactions which all men have to the same objects; he means rather to assert that a measure of such uniformity in fact exists.

In any case, there is a sharp difference between Hume's position and Professor Findlay's about the significance of such uniformities as our responses exhibit. Hume explicitly traces them to the 'structure of the internal fabric'; whereas Professor Findlay considers it a weakness in both eighteenth- and twentieth-century 'sentimentalists' that when they admit a certain constancy in our emotions and attitudes in given situations, they have 'tended to ascribe this to some merely constitutional bias, to some accident of our human make-up'[2] —he claims that his own 'truth' and 'falsehood' in emotions is something more purely objective than this. One of his grounds for making this claim, at least in the case of ethical emotions, would appear to be that, for him, the existing uniformities in such responses are not just unexplained brute facts—they have come about because we *want* our ethical responses to be uniform; it is, in fact, part of the definition of an 'ethical response' that it is one which we want to be made by all men, and one about which we are prepared to make adjustments in order to secure their concurrence.

'Men's moral attitudes must, in consequence of their nature

[1] *Essays; Of the Standard of Taste.*   [2] Op. cit., p. 147.

and their mode of testing, tend steadily towards an ever higher level of agreement. However varied they may be at first, the process of social attrition to which they are continuously subjected must necessarily leave them highly uniform.'[1]

Hume, however, was not unaware of this process. For him, the 'impartiality' of approval and disapproval is closely bound up with our desire both that these reactions should remain stable throughout our own changes of situation, and that they should be shared by others.

'Our situation with regard both to persons and things is in continual fluctuation; and a man that lies at a distance from us may in a little time become a familiar acquaintance. Besides, every particular man has a peculiar position with regard to others; and it is impossible we could ever converse together on any reasonable terms, were each of us to consider characters and persons only as they appear from his peculiar point of view. In order, therefore, to prevent those continual *contradictions*, and arrive at a more *stable* judgment of things, we fix on some *steady* and *general* points of view, and always, in our thoughts, place ourselves in them, whatever may be our present situation.'[2]

And the only standpoint which 'appears the same to every spectator' is a position *close* to that of the agent we are judging. The effect of this adoption of a common imaginary standpoint, coupled with the constant interchange of moral opinions, is a widespread agreement in our considered moral judgements. 'The intercourse of sentiments, . . . in society and conversation, makes us form some general unalterable standard, by which we may approve or disapprove of character and manners.'[3] It is, nevertheless, clear to Hume that this process of 'social attrition', and the associated process of divesting ourselves of partiality, cannot eliminate all dependence of the character of the ultimately prevailing ethical responses upon the 'structure of the internal fabric'—upon the 'accidents', the 'constitutional bias', of 'our human make-

[1] p. 160.   [2] *Treatise*, III. iii. 1.   [3] *Enquiry*, v. ii.

up'. For it is just the brute fact of the human emotional constitution which determines *what* men will feel when they take up the position of disinterested acquaintances of the agent, and what responses they will be prepared to try and alter for the sake of uniformity, and so what ones will be established after the long process of mutual adjustment. It is, indeed, 'impossible for such a creature as man to be totally indifferent to the well or ill-being of his fellow creatures, and not readily, of himself, to pronounce, where nothing gives him any particular bias, that what promotes their happiness is good, what tends to their misery is evil'; but we can only conclude this from 'the principles of the human make, such as they appear to daily experience and observation'.[1] And even so, there are differences on points of detail. Hume says that we all 'reap a pleasure from the view of a character which is naturally fitted to be useful to others, or to the person himself, or which is agreeable to others, or to the person himself';[2] but he says nothing about the proportionate merits we attach to these qualities, and does not suggest that there would be universal agreement on that point. On 'taste' more generally, he is quite clear that 'the different humours of particular men', though 'not sufficient indeed to confound all the boundaries of beauty and deformity', will nevertheless 'often serve to produce a difference in the degrees of our approbation and blame'; and in such case 'we seek in vain for a standard, by which we can reconcile the contrary sentiments'.[3]

The same point is clear in Smith. He too begins from our desire for community in sentiment with others, pointing out that this not only leads us to 'disapprove' of reactions which are not what ours would have been, but also to attempt to modify our own.

'Mankind, though naturally sympathetic, never conceive, for what has befallen another, that degree of passion which naturally animates the person principally concerned. . . . The person

[1] Ibid. [2] *Treatise*, III. iii. 1. [3] *Of the Standard of Taste.*

principally concerned is sensible of this, and at the same time passionately desires a more complete sympathy. . . . But he can only hope to obtain this by lowering his passion to that pitch, in which the spectators are capable of going along with him.'[1]

This necessity, according to Smith, is the source of all those virtues which we sum up under the name of 'self-command'; and also of self-criticism.

'We either approve or disapprove of our own conduct, according as we feel that, when we place ourselves in the situation of another man, and view it, as it were, with his eyes and from his station, we either can or cannot entirely enter into and sympathise with the sentiments and motives which influenced it.'[2]

But the adoption of such a detached standpoint only removes one of the obvious sources of divergence in men's reactions, namely, self-interest, as careful consideration of all the circumstances may remove another; but even after that, moral tastes may still differ. And, while such self-criticism from a spectator's standpoint is first undertaken in order to anticipate the judgement of others and so secure, at least, a secondary conformity between our sentiments and theirs, we soon come to seek the approval of the 'impartial spectator' within —our own 'critical self'—*instead of* that of other real people.

'When we first come into the world, from the natural desire to please, we accustom ourselves to consider what behaviour is likely to be agreeable to every person we converse with. . . . We are soon taught by experience, however, that this universal approbation is altogether unattainable', and so come to 'set up in our own minds a judge between ourselves and those we live with. We conceive ourselves as acting in the presence of . . . an impartial spectator who considers our conduct with the same indifference with which we regard that of other people. If, when we place ourselves in the situation of such a person, our own actions appear to us under an agreeable aspect, . . . whatever be the judgments of the world, we must still be pleased with our own behaviour.'[3]

[1] *Moral Sentiments*, I. i. 4.   [2] III. i.   [3] First edition, III. ii.

Nor is this merely an appeal to the 'great company of reflective people' who have examined our motives and circumstances as 'present company' have not. The distinction between ignorant and discerning praise or blame *is* important, since 'the man who applauds us either for actions which we did not perform, or for motives which had no sort of influence upon our conduct, applauds not us, but another person'.[1] But Smith still distinguishes not only between 'what are' and 'what, upon a certain condition, would be' the judgement of others (the 'condition' being perfect knowledge of our motives and circumstances), but also between the latter and 'what, we imagine, ought to be the judgment of others'.[2] 'What, we imagine, ought to be the judgment of others' is, of course, simply what ours would be if we were in their place. Every man is endowed 'not only with a desire of being approved of, but with a desire of being what ought to be approved of; *or of being what he himself approves of in other men*' (italics mine).[3]

Smith's final word, even here, thus directs us to his undisguisedly subjective notion of 'propriety', as reacting in the same way as we would in the like situation (this time, in that of a spectator). But we have seen in an earlier study that, in his first account of this notion, Smith takes over from Hume's general theory of knowledge a confusion between feeling and opinion from which Hume himself is free when he handles the special topic of the moral consciousness. Professor Findlay's relation to Smith seems at this point to be very like Smith's to Hume. In his handling of the modification of our moral sentiments caused by our desire that others should share them, Smith forgets about his unfortunate comparison between the propriety of a feeling and the truth of an opinion. He nowhere suggests that the concurrence of others in our moral sentiments makes those sentiments 'true'. But just this suggestion, as we have seen, is made by Professor Findlay.

[1] Final edition, III. ii.   [2] III. i.   [3] III. ii.

As in the simpler case which misled Smith, there is a certain superficial resemblance between the 'tests' which Professor Findlay would have us apply to our primary ethical responses and the procedures by which we test the truth of a judgement. For in the latter case also, we can only, in the end, survey the facts more and more carefully, clear our minds of prejudice, and 'compare notes' with other people. (This is true, at least, of judgements not arrived at by inference.) And if we take a rationalistic or objectivist view of ethics, and hold that our primary ethical responses *are* judgements in the strictest sense—judgements as to whether or not an action or disposition really possesses such properties as rightness or wrongness, or the relational property of moral appropriateness—then these are the only ways in which we can test the truth of our immediate moral judgements (i.e. ones not inferred from others, and presupposed by inferred ones). We find the test of 'reflection' emphasized, for instance, by Mr. Carritt, when he says that all we can do to persuade a man of the rightness or wrongness of some action is to

'give him fuller information of the consequences and antecedents of what he is doing and then ask him to agree with you that it is right or wrong. If he know the situation and consequences as well as you do and still differ . . . all you can do is to get him to imagine the situation again and repeat the act of moral thinking with greater attention.'[1]

And this is also—as Professor Prichard hints[2]—all we can do to settle *our own* doubts. Sidgwick emphasizes the function of such attentive consideration in clearing our minds of prejudice.

'Most persons are liable to confound intuitions, on the one hand with mere impressions and impulses, which to careful observation do not present themselves as claiming to be dictates of Reason; and on the other hand, with mere opinions, to which the familiarity that comes from frequent hearing and repetition

[1] *The Theory of Morals*, p. 72.   [2] *Mind*, 1912, pp. 34–7.

often gives a false appearance of self-evidence which attentive reflection disperses.'

Sidgwick also gives the most accurate account of the precise bearing of comparison with the results obtained by other people upon the validity of our moral intuitions.

'Since it is implied in the very notion of Truth that it is essentially the same for all minds, the denial by another of a proposition that I have affirmed has a tendency to impair my confidence in its validity. . . . For if I find any of my judgments, intuitive or inferential, in direct conflict with a judgment of some other mind, there must be error somewhere: and if I have no more reason to suspect error in the other mind than in my own, reflective comparison between the two judgments necessarily reduces me temporarily to a state of neutrality. And though the total result in my own mind is not exactly suspense of judgment, but an alternation and conflict between positive affirmation by one act of thought and the neutrality that is the result of another, it is obviously something very different from scientific certitude.'[1]

But Professor Findlay's employment of these tests really has a totally different purpose. The only thing about the ethical response which the process of reflection tests, or is meant to test, is whether it really will survive the process of reflection; and the only thing about it which the process of 'social attrition' tests is whether it really will secure general acceptance, i.e. whether it really will survive the process of 'social attrition'. They are tests of the capacity of the response to survive the tests, and of nothing more than that. On the other hand, when they are used as tests of the truth of genuine judgements, what they are testing *is* something more than the capacity of the judgements to survive the tests. For the truth of a judgement is something more than its power to survive the inspection of the facts—it is its *accordance* with the facts—and something more than its power to command general assent—namely, again, its accordance with

[1] *The Methods of Ethics*, III. xi. 2.

the facts, about which it is supposed, rightly or wrongly, that a majority of careful observers are not likely to be mistaken.

We may approach the matter in another way. It is a very important part of Professor Findlay's technique to define ethical responses as ones which we are prepared to have tested in these ways—he says that we simply would not *call* a response an ethical one if the person making it were not prepared to submit it to such and such a test. And we must admit that this procedure, like all 'naturalistic' definition of key ethical concepts, is legitimate, in so far as men, and also societies and cultures and schools of thought, may use words as they please. But, as Professor Moore insists, whoever lays down a definition must be prepared to accept its consequences. Now Professor Findlay tells us at one point that 'the moral sphere is really one of these spheres in which the *orbis terrarum* may be said to judge securely'.[1] But since he defines an ethical response as one in which we are prepared to submit to the decision of the *orbis terrarum*, this is simply a tautology. And I do not think Professor Findlay would attempt to deny that it is; but one further consequence of its being a tautology which he appears to have overlooked is that it makes his employment of this particular test for the 'truth' of an ethical response differ *in toto* from its employment as a test of the truth of a judgement. For if it is a fact that the *orbis terrarum* judges securely on questions of truth and falsehood (as those terms are ordinarily understood), then it is a highly significant fact, and not the mere tautology that the *orbis terrarum* judges as it does. And conversely, if it is a mere tautology that the *orbis terrarum* judges securely in moral matters, then this 'judgement' is not one of truth and falsehood, in any ordinary sense of those terms.

[1] p. 160.

IX

THE NATURALISTIC FALLACY:
THE HISTORY OF ITS REFUTATION

WE have seen that the claim to infer significant ethical propositions from definitions of ethical terms, which appears to
constitute the essence of what Professor Moore calls the
naturalistic fallacy, is a special case of a more general fallacious claim, namely, the claim to deduce ethical propositions
from ones which are admitted to be non-ethical. We have
considered some of the forms in which this claim has been
historically put forward, and some of the ways in which it has
been historically refuted. We have also considered attempts
to give ethics a 'foundation' by misleading extensions of the
concept of 'truth', and the ways in which the fallacies involved in such attempts have been or may be exposed. All
this has provided us with a broad context in which we can
study the history of the exposure, by the method which we
now think of as Professor Moore's, of the naturalistic
fallacy itself.

The closest approach to an anticipation of Professor Moore
that we have yet encountered is perhaps Cudworth's relega-
tion to a parenthesis, as something which his opponents
cannot have seriously meant to maintain, of the view that
good and evil are 'mere names without signification, or names
for nothing else but willed and commanded'. But Cudworth
does not explain why he considers this possibility out of the
question. Here and there, however, among those who came
after Cudworth, there are to be found writers who do consider it worth while to explain why this possibility cannot be
seriously entertained. The earliest of such explanations which
I have been able to trace is that of Shaftesbury, who points
out that 'whoever thinks there is a God, and pretends

formally to believe that he is just and good, must suppose that there is independently such a thing as justice and injustice, truth and falsehood, right and wrong, according to which he pronounces that God is just, righteous, and true. If the mere will, decree, or law of God be said absolutely to constitute right or wrong, then are these latter words'—i.e. the 'pronouncement' that God is just, righteous, and true—'of no significancy at all'.[1] And the anticipation of Moore is made complete a little later by Hutcheson, who writes: 'To call the laws of the Supreme Deity good, or holy, or just, if all goodness, holiness and justice be constituted by laws, or by the will of a superior any way revealed, must be an insignificant tautology, amounting to no more than this, "That God wills what he wills".'[2]

The inconsistent ethical naturalist whom Shaftesbury and Hutcheson had chiefly in mind when formulating their criticism was probably John Locke.

'Things are good and evil', Locke held, 'only in reference to pleasure and pain. That we call good, which is apt to cause or increase pleasure, or diminish pain in us; or else to procure or preserve us the possession of any other good or absence of any evil. And, on the contrary, we name that evil which is apt to produce or increase any pain, or diminish any pleasure in us; or else to procure us any evil, or deprive us of any good.'[3]

And again, 'Good and evil . . . are nothing but pleasure and pain, or that which occasions or procures pleasure or pain to us.'[4] 'Moral' good or evil is a special kind of source of pleasure and pain, namely, 'the conformity or disagreement of our voluntary actions to some law, whereby good or evil'— i.e. pleasure or pain—'is drawn on us by the will and power

[1] *An Inquiry concerning Virtue*, Bk. I, Part III, sect. ii.
[2] *An Inquiry concerning the Original of our Ideas of Virtue and Moral Good*, VII. v; Selby-Bigge, 173. I have drawn attention to this passage, and to the one from Shaftesbury, in the *Australasian Journal of Psychology and Philosophy*, December 1946, p. 172.
[3] *Essay concerning Human Understanding*, II. xx. 2.   [4] II. xxviii. 5.

of the law-maker'.[1] And the law which determines what actions are 'sins or duties' (and not merely 'criminal or innocent' in the eyes of one's government, or proper or improper in the eyes of one's society) is the law or command-ment of God.[2] Here is 'naturalism' at its purest—'moral' good and evil (right and wrong) reduced to a form or function of 'natural' good and evil (pleasure and pain) in so many words. And Locke is consistent enough to recognize that this makes some propositions about our duty tautologous, or almost so.

'If virtue be taken for actions conformable to God's will, or to the rule prescribed by God, which is the true and only measure of virtue when virtue is used to signify what is in its own nature right and good: then this proposition, "That virtue is the best worship of God", will be most true and certain, but of very little use in human life, since it will amount to no more but this, viz. "That God is pleased with the doing of what he commands"; which a man may certainly know to be true, without knowing what it is that God doth command, and so be as far from any rule or principle of his actions as he was before.'[3]

This is directed against Lord Herbert of Cherbury's claim that the proposition in question is a self-evident ethical prin-ciple; Locke in effect admits its self-evidence, but denies its status as an ethical principle. Yet Locke can also say that God has a 'right' to rule us, and that not only because He has power to enforce His commands 'by rewards and punish-ments of infinite weight and duration', but also because 'he has goodness and wisdom to direct our actions to that which is best'.[4] Does God's 'goodness' here mean merely that He is a source of pleasure? If so, He is also 'evil', as being, to the disobedient, a source of pain. Or is His goodness 'moral'? Then it means, as Hutcheson says, no more than that His will accords with itself. And does His 'right' to impose laws mean that it is in accordance with His laws that He should

[1] Ibid.   [2] II. xxviii. 7.   [3] I. iii. 18.   [4] II. xxviii. 8.

impose them? This also seems to tell us no more than that He commands what He commands.

In the middle of the eighteenth century this criticism was explicitly directed against Locke by Richard Price. '*Mr. Locke* . . . represents *rectitude* as signifying conformity of actions to some rules or laws; which rules or laws, he says, are either *the will of God*, the decrees of the magistrate, or *the fashion of the country*: From whence it follows, that it is an absurdity to apply *rectitude* to rules and laws themselves' or 'to suppose the *divine* will to be directed by it.' 'But', he adds, 'it is undoubted that this great man would have detested these consequences; and, indeed, it is sufficiently evident, that he was strangely embarrassed in his notions on this, as well as some other subjects.'[1] Price makes a similar criticism of Bishop Warburton, who 'maintains, that moral obligation always denotes some object of will and law, and implies some obliger. Were this true, it would be mere jargon to mention our being obliged to obey the Divine will; and yet, this is as proper language as any we can use.'[2] These are, of course, mere hints of Professor Moore's argument from trivialization, like the hint in Shaftesbury; not full anticipations of it, like that in Hutcheson. But the latter may be found in Price too; in fact, no other writer has anticipated Professor Moore quite so completely.[3]

This more complete anticipation occurs, curiously enough, in a section[4] in which Price's main purpose is to state his difference from Hutcheson; though it occurs there as a digression. Their difference concerns what Price calls 'the Foundation of Morals'. On Hutcheson's view (which Price identifies perhaps too unreservedly with Hume's), 'moral right and wrong, signify nothing *in the objects* themselves to which they

[1] *Review*, p. 43; Selby-Bigge, 609.
[2] *Review*, p. 116; Selby-Bigge, 684.
[3] The first person to have noticed this, so far as I am aware, was Dr. Raphael. See *The Moral Sense*, pp. 1, 111 ff.
[4] *Review*, I. i.

are applied, any more than agreeable and harsh', and 'our perception of *right*, or moral good, in actions, is that agreeable *emotion*, or feeling, which certain actions produce in us: and of wrong, the contrary'.[1]

'The present enquiry therefore is; whether this be a true account of virtue or not; whether it *has* or has *not* a foundation in the *nature* of its object; whether *right* and *wrong* are real characters of *actions*, or only qualities of our *minds*; whether, in short, they denote what actions *are*, or only *sensations* derived from the particular frame and structure of our natures.'

But there is one set of theories—'the schemes which found morality on self-love, on positive laws and compacts, or the Divine will'—which may not seem to fit very well into either of these pigeon-holes. But these 'must either mean, that moral good and evil are only other words for *advantageous* and *disadvantageous*, *willed* and *forbidden*. Or they relate to a different question; that is, not to the question, what is the nature and true *account* of virtue; but what is the *subject-matter* of it.'[2] If the latter is their meaning—if they mean that being advantageous to the agent, or being commanded by God or by some other authority, are the only charac-teristics of actions which *make* them right—then what they have to say has no bearing on the question as to what broad kind or category of quality 'rightness' itself is. On the other hand, if the key propositions of these schemes are intended as definitions, the consequence of accepting them would be that 'it would be palpably absurd in any case to ask, whether it be right to obey a command, or wrong to disobey it; and the propositions, obeying a command is right, or pro-ducing happiness is right, would be most trifling, as express-ing no more than that obeying a command, is obeying a command, or producing happiness, is producing happiness'.[3] Here we have Professor Moore's whole armoury—not only

[1] Selby-Bigge, 585. [2] Ibid., 586.
[3] Ibid., 587.

the argument from trivialization, but the distinction under-
lying it, between a definition of a moral term, and a significant
ethical generalization.

Views akin to Locke's found a number of adherents among
the eighteenth-century clergy. Fielding's *Tom Jones* contains
a number of debates between one such clergyman, who is
given the name of 'Thwackum', and a person called 'Square',
who is of the school of Clarke (Fielding himself fairly plainly
writes from the point of view of Shaftesbury—a moderate
'sentimentalism', more concerned to insist upon the reality
of generous emotions in men than to propound any theory of
the nature of the moral faculty). In 1785 this 'theological
naturalism' was given its classical form in Paley's *Principles
of Moral and Political Philosophy*. Paley defines virtue as 'the
doing good to mankind, in obedience to the will of God, and
for the sake of everlasting happiness';[1] 'right' as 'consistency
with the will of God';[2] and 'obligation' as being 'urged by
a violent motive resulting from the command of another'.[3]
If it is asked, 'Why am I *obliged* to keep my word?' on this
system, 'the answer will be, "because I am urged to do so by
a violent motive" (namely the expectation of being after this
life rewarded, if I do, or punished for it if I do not), "resulting
from the command of another" (namely of God)'. 'This
solution', Paley complacently comments, 'goes to the bottom
of the subject, as no further question can reasonably be asked.
. . . Private happiness is our motive, and the will of God
our rule.'[4]

In a note[5] to the final edition of his *Review*, Price makes
the comment on this that might have been expected from him.
'Mr. PALEY's definition of RIGHT is, "the being consistent
with the will of God". RECTITUDE, therefore, can be no guide
to God's will itself; and to say that his will is a righteous will,
is the same with saying that his will is his will.' The same
consequence of Paley's position is emphasized in the critical

---

[1] I. vii.   [2] II. ix.   [3] II. ii.   [4] II. iii.   [5] Note F.

annotations to the edition of the *Moral and Political Philosophy* which was produced in the middle of last century by Archbishop Whately, the logician. Whately notes, to begin with, that if a man 'attaches no meaning to the words "good", and "just", and "right", except that such is the divine command, then, to say that God is good, and his commands just, is only saying in a circuitous way, that He is what He is, and that what He wills He wills, which might be said of any Being in the universe'.[1] Whately, as a theist, admits that

'we do conclude in this or that *particular instance*, that so and so is wise and good, though we do not perceive its wisdom and goodness, but found our conviction solely on its being the divine will. But then, this is from our general *conviction* that God *is* wise and good; not from our attaching no meaning to the words wise and good, except the divine will. . . . And so it is in many other cases. You have read (suppose) several works of a certain author, and have found them all highly interesting and instructive. If, then, you hear of his bringing out a new work, you expect, before you have seen it, that it will be a valuable one. But this is not from your meaning by a "valuable work" nothing at all but that it comes from his pen.'[2]

'It is true . . . that we are *commanded* to do what is right, and forbidden to do what is wrong,' but 'it is not true that this is the only meaning of the words "right" and "wrong." And it is true that God *will* reward and punish', but not 'that a calculation of reward and punishment constitutes the whole notion of Duty.'[3] Paley, in short, identifies goodness with characteristics which are merely its invariable and necessary accompaniments.

The 'argument from trivialization' was a favourite one with Whately. It occurs in his *Lessons on Morals*, which appeared in 1855, four years before the edition of Paley; and may be found also in a letter written a year before that, in which he says, referring to those who say that 'right' means commanded by God:

'One might ask one of these moral teachers, "Do you think it right to obey the Divine will?" . . . do you think that God has a just claim on your obedience? For, if you do, then to say that it is "morally right" to obey Him, and yet that all our notions of morality are derived from our notions of His will, is just to say that what He has commanded is—what He has commanded!'[1]

Paley could, of course, have avoided any charge of circularity by simply denying that there is any meaning in such assertions as that God is just, or that it is right to obey Him. He could have said that since God has power to enforce His commands, the fact that it is merely tautological to call them just does not matter. And indeed he comes very close to saying precisely this when he tells us that the appeal to self-interest takes us to 'the bottom of the subject', and that 'no further question can reasonably be asked'. But he is not quite consistent about this; the position he takes up is, in fact, rather remarkable. Immediately after having defined 'right' as 'consistency with the will of God', he himself raises the question, 'But if the divine will determine the distinction of right and wrong, what else is it but an identical proposition to say of God, that He acts *right*? or how is it possible to conceive even that He should act wrong? Yet these assertions are intelligible and significant.' Archbishop Whately, or Professor Moore, could not have said more; how, then, does Paley escape?

'The case', he says, 'is thus: By virtue of the two principles. that God wills the happiness of his creatures, and that the will of God is the measure of right and wrong, we arrive at certain conclusions; which conclusions become rules; and we soon learn to pronounce actions right or wrong, according as they agree or disagree with our rules, without looking any further; and when the habit is once established of stopping at the rules, we can go

---

[1] *Life of Archbishop Whately*, vol. ii, p. 314.

back and compare with these rules the divine conduct itself: and yet it may be true (only not observed by us at the time) that the rules themselves are deduced from the divine will.'

'Arguing in a *circle*', Whately comments on this, 'is very common; with crafty sophists, from design, and with bad reasoners, from confusion of thought. But the former are very careful to conceal the fallacy; and the latter do not perceive it. It is very strange that Paley should perceive and acknowledge that he is involved in a circle, and should yet adhere to it.'[1] There does not seem to be anything that one could add to this or take away from it. And yet—*has* Paley argued in a circle here? Paley was, in his time, a Cambridge philosopher; and had he been a Cambridge philosopher in our time he might have answered his own question in some such way as this: 'We can intelligibly ask whether what God does and commands is right, and we can intelligibly ask whether what produces happiness is right. But this does not mean that in each case we are asking whether the subject possesses some possibly "non-natural" predicate distinct from both "conforming to God's will" and "productive of happiness". There is no such thing as *the* meaning of "right". The acts which we have learnt to describe so are in fact both done and commanded by God, and productive of happiness. And when we ask whether what God wills is right, we are asking whether all God's deeds and commands are like these ones in promoting happiness; while when we ask whether promoting happiness is good, we are asking whether all felicific actions are like these ones in being done or commanded by God.' And is this so very different from what Paley actually said?

At all events, what Paley said at this point was in part an unconscious prophecy. His *Moral and Political Philosophy* first appeared a few years after Bentham's *Principles of Morals and Legislation*; but Paley crystallized the theological

[1] p. 88.

Utilitarianism of the preceding period, while Bentham's secular Utilitarianism caught the ear of the age which followed it. And whereas the older school had defined virtue as obedience to the will of God, and made the promotion of happiness its 'subject-matter', in Bentham the latter became the definition.

'Of an action that is conformable to the principle of utility one may always say either that it is one that ought to be done, or at least that it is not one that ought not to be done. One may say also that it is right it should be done; at least that it is not wrong it should be done. . . . When thus interpreted, the words *ought*, and *right* and *wrong*, and others of that stamp, have a meaning; when otherwise they have none.'[1]

But he goes on immediately to treat the 'principle of utility'— that is, 'that principle which approves or disapproves of any action whatsoever, according to the tendency which it appears to have . . . to promote or oppose happiness'[2]—not as a mere definition, but as the self-evident premiss of all true and significant moral propositions. 'Is it susceptible of direct proof? it should seem not: for that which is used to prove everything else, cannot itself be proved. . . . To give such proof is as impossible as it is needless.'[3] And Bentham could not have given Paley's answer to the charge that he was guilty of the naturalistic fallacy at this point; for in him, although the promotion of happiness takes the place of obedience to God's will as the definition of right action, obedience to God's will does not take the place of promoting happiness as the 'subject-matter' of it, but simply disappears. Bentham has not, that is to say, a definition and a rule distinct from the definition which may, through a natural shift of usage, change places with it; in him the definition and the rule are one.

So far as I am aware, the first writer to charge Bentham, in effect, with committing the naturalistic fallacy was Sidgwick, though he found it hard to believe that Bentham's

[1] *Principles of Morals and Legislation*, I. x.   [2] I. ii.   [3] I. xi.

identification of his rule and his definition was seriously intended. His criticism occurs in a brief footnote,[1] where he argues that

'when Bentham explains . . . that his fundamental principle "states the greatest happiness of all those whose interest is in question as being the right and proper end of human action", we cannot understand him really to *mean* by the word "right" "conducive to the general happiness", though his language in other passages of the same chapter . . . would seem to imply this; for the proposition that it is conducive to general happiness to take general happiness as an end of action, though not exactly a tautology, can hardly serve as the fundamental principle of a moral system.' [It is not 'exactly' a tautology because to aim at some end is not necessarily the best way of actually realising it.]

This note is given simply as illustrating the point that the description of something as 'right' cannot always mean merely that it is the fittest means to some end, because we sometimes 'regard as "right" the adoption of certain ends—such as the common good of society, or the general happiness'. It is a note of considerable historical importance, as there is good reason to believe that it inspired Professor Moore's work on the 'naturalistic fallacy'. It is cited in a section in which Professor Moore begins by saying that, so far as he knows, 'there is only one ethical writer, Prof. Henry Sidgwick, who has clearly recognized and stated' the fact that 'good' is indefinable.[2]

Sidgwick would certainly have been the last to have claimed any originality for himself at this point. In his *History* the first point which he notices in his account of Price is 'his conception of "right" and "wrong" as "single ideas" incapable of definition or analysis'. (I suspect that 'single' here is a misprint for 'simple'.) Nor, I should say, did he imagine that he was original in his use of the 'argument from trivialization', apart from his being the first (if he was the

[1] To *The Methods of Ethics*, I. iii. 1.   [2] *Principia Ethica*, p. 17.

first) to apply it to the particular case of Bentham. He was familiar with the work of Shaftesbury, Hutcheson, and Price, and would know the passage from Shaftesbury not only directly, but also as quoted against Paley in Dugald Stewart's *Philosophy of the Active and Moral Powers of Man*,[1] a work which he regarded as 'a lucid, comprehensive, and judicious attempt to put together the elements of truth in the work of preceding writers, including Shaftesbury and Adam Smith, into a harmonious and coherent statement of the results of impartial reflection on the moral consciousness'.[2] (Three writers of the period before Sidgwick's—Price, Stewart, and Whately—have now been mentioned as using the argument from trivialization against Paley; and it seems not unlikely that others did so too, particularly since Paley himself admitted that it might be raised.)

Sidgwick came still closer to the language of Professor Moore in a work published posthumously only a year before the first appearance of the *Principia Ethica*, on *The Ethics of Green, Spencer, and Martineau*. In the second lecture on Spencer, the latter's contention that ' "pleasurable" and "painful"are the primary meanings of "good" and "bad" ' is met with the observation that

'we must distinguish inquiry into the meaning of words from inquiry into ethical principles. I agree with Mr. Spencer in holding that "pleasure is the ultimate good", but not in the meaning which he gives to the word "good". Indeed, if "good" (substantive) means "pleasure", the proposition just stated would be a tautology, and a tautology cannot be an ethical principle.'[3]

There is, in fact, a far-reaching similarity in aim, or shall we say in provocation, between this work of Sidgwick's and the *Principia Ethica*, as both books attempt to show that the evolutionary ethical naturalism of Spencer and the 'metaphysical' ethics of T. H. Green suffer from a common error.

---

[1] II. v. I.   [2] *History of Ethics*, ch. iv.
[3] *Ethics of Green*, &c., p. 145.

Professor Moore identifies this common error with the 'naturalistic fallacy'; but although Sidgwick, as we have just seen, does mention this in connexion with Spencer, he treats it, as we have earlier suggested it ought to be treated, as an element in a larger error, namely, the denial of the autonomy of Ethics.

'Spencer and Green', he says in his opening paragraph, 'represent two lines of thought divergent from my own in opposite directions, but agreeing in that they do not treat Ethics as a subject that can stand alone. Spencer bases it on Science, Green on Metaphysics. In discussing Spencer', he goes on, 'we shall be dealing with an attempt to "establish Ethics on a scientific basis". Now this, I hold, cannot be done to the extent and in the manner in which Mr. Spencer tries to do it. "Science" relates to what is, has been and will be, Ethics to what ought to be; therefore the fundamental principles of the latter must be independent of the former, however important and even indispensable Science—especially Biology and Sociology—may be in the working out of the system of rules. And Science—in particular Psychology and Sociology—may trace the origin of moral sentiments and ideas, but it cannot itself supply a criterion of the validity of moral principles, or authority of moral sentiments.'

With this last point, as it has been developed both by Sidgwick and by other writers, we have already dealt quite fully. Nor need any more be said in order to establish the fact that Professor Moore's achievement has not been to work a revolution in Moral Philosophy, but simply to help keep alive, in our own age, the eighteenth-century tradition of sanity and logical rigour which Sidgwick (with Huxley the agnostic beside him and Whately the Archbishop behind him) kept alive in his.

NOTE A

AMONG earlier rationalists, there was a hint of this in Balguy. 'As ideas themselves are of various kinds, so the Relations interceding between them are conformably different. . . . Can then such an Equality or Proportion . . . be ascribed to . . . Moral Ideas', i.e. to the characters of actions and of the experiences provoking them, 'as belongs to . . . Mathematical ones? Those Terms,' i.e. Equality and Proportion, 'are used and applied to both kinds, but not precisely in the same sense. They belong originally to Ideas of Quantity; and when they are used to denote Moral Fitness, their Signification is somewhat figurative' (Selby-Bigge, 714–15). But Balguy (see Note C) did not keep this up. (*See p. 58.*)

NOTE B

IT is this fact alone which makes it possible for commands and prohibitions to be related in such logical or quasi-logical ways as those indicated by Mr. R. M. Hare in his article on 'Imperative Sentences' in *Mind* for January 1949. (*See p. 71.*)

NOTE C

THE term 'validity' is ordinarily applied neither to a statement nor to a command, but to a process of reasoning; and in a paper on *The Moral Problem* by Reginald Jackson, published posthumously in *Mind* for October 1948, it is suggested that responsible choice is a form of reasoning, so that validity and invalidity may be predicated of it quite literally. 'To reason is simply to be guided by judgement', and the species of reasoning are 'judgement guided by judgement', or inference, and 'conduct guided by judgement', or responsible choice (p. 442). In other words, to judge that a man has done something for which we contracted to pay him sixpence is to have a reason for paying it to him, in exactly the same sense of 'having a reason' as to judge that all men are mortal and Socrates is a man is to have a reason for judging that Socrates is mortal. (For an eighteenth-century parallel, see Balguy's answer, in Selby-Bigge, 717, to the question as to how we may 'deduce the particular Obligation to gratitude' from the mere 'ideas' of gratitude and bounty, the 'idea' of obligation not being given independently: 'If receiving of Benefits be a good Reason, as it certainly is, why the Receiver should be grateful, then it obliges him so to be. . . . Every Man who receives a Benefit, receives along with it a Reason for Gratitude.') But I should say that 'having a reason' can only bear the same sense in these two cases if actions share with judgements the capacity for truth and falsity; for to have a reason for judging that Socrates is mortal is simply to have made some judgement which cannot be true unless the judgement that Socrates is mortal is true. Jackson's theory presupposes Wollaston's. (*See p. 76.*)

NOTE D

WOLLASTON, anticipating an objection of this sort, asks, 'If it be *natural* to conclude any thing' from actions, 'do they not *naturally* convey the notice of something to be concluded? And what is conveying the *notice* of any thing but *notifying* or signifying that thing?' (*Religion of Nature*, I. iii.) But a proposition does not 'signify', in the sense in which its 'signifying' locates the fact which renders it true or false, all that it is 'natural' to conclude from it on the basis of common experience. If it did, it would be impossible to signify by propositions the facts which sometimes lead us to revise our 'natural' generalizations, and these generalizations themselves would become mere identities (cf. Keynes, *Formal Logic*, p. 55, n. 1. It is plain that the only sort of 'meaning' that actions can have, except when they form an arranged system of signals, is something analogous to what Dr. Keynes, discussing the denotation and connotation of names, distinguishes from their conventionally fixed connotation as their 'subjective intension', i.e. all the qualities which our experience causes to be 'normally called up in idea when a name is used'. Conversely, it is only in some such sense that the indicative sentence, 'A scorpion has just crawled up your trousers', has the hearer's impulse to take off his trousers as part of its 'meaning', as Mr. R. M. Hare implies that it has, in *Mind*, January, 1949, p. 39.) (*See p. 84.*)

GENERAL NOTE

ONE of the first rationalist replies to Hutcheson, John Balguy's *Foundation of Moral Goodness* (1728), contains a suggestion that the Glasgow moralist's use of the 'argument from trivialization' may be turned against himself. The way in which the suggestion arises is as follows: Hutcheson was aware that his view that the root of all virtue lies in generous instincts, and of all approval in an equally instinctive preference, was open to the objection that in that case we cannot be sure that God will not some day give us quite different instincts. Hutcheson's reply was that God may be trusted in this matter because He would not have implanted these instincts in us in the first place if He did not have 'affections' of substantially the same sort Himself. At this point Balguy meets Hutcheson's answer with the further query, 'Is such a Disposition a Perfection in the Deity, or is it not? Is it better than a contrary, or than any other Disposition would have been?' (Selby-Bigge, *British Moralists*, 528.) And the fact that this question is intelligible indicates that Hutcheson's criticism of the view that 'all goodness, holiness and justice is constituted by laws' may be retorted upon himself. 'Our Author . . . has made the following Observation. That our first Ideas of moral Good depend not on laws, may plainly appear from our constant Enquiries into the Justice of Laws themselves; and that not only of human Laws, but also of the Divine. What else can be the Meaning of that universal Opinion, that Laws of God are just, and holy, and good? Very right. But I wonder much this Sentiment should not have led the Author to the true original Idea of Moral Goodness. For after we have made such Enquiries, do we find Reason to conclude that any Laws are good, merely from their being conformable to the Affections of the Legislator? And in respect of the divine Laws, what is it that convinces us that they are just, and holy, and good? Is it their Conformity to a certain Disposition which we suppose in the Deity? . . . If we impartially consult our Ideas, I am persuaded we shall find that moral Goodness no more depends originally on Affections and Dispositions, than it does on Laws; and that there is something in Actions, absolutely good, antecedent to both' (529). Balguy's recommendation that we 'impartially consult our Ideas' is equivalent to Professor Moore's that we 'attentively consider' whether, in the case of any given X, the question 'Is X good?', and the answer that it is, have any meaning; and his conclusion is that it is as significant to say that God's 'affections' are righteous, or that ours are, as it is to say that His (or our) commands are.